LISBON
in your pocket

MICHELIN
Travel Publications

MANUFACTURE FRANÇAISE DES PNEUMATIQUES MICHELIN

Place des Carmes-Déchaux – 63000 Clermont-Ferrand (France)

© Michelin et Cie. Propriétaires-Éditeurs 1998

Dêpôt légal Avril 98 – ISBN 2-06-652301-1 – ISSN 1272-1689

No part of this publication may be reproduced in any form without the prior permission of the publisher.

Printed in Spain 5-00/2

MICHELIN TRAVEL PUBLICATIONS
Michelin Tyre plc
The Edward Hyde Building
38 Clarendon Road
WATFORD Herts WD1 1SX - UK
☎ (01923) 415000
www.michelin-travel.com

MICHELIN TRAVEL PUBLICATIONS
Michelin North America
One Parkway South
GREENVILLE, SC 29615
☎ 1-800 423-0485
www.michelin-travel.com

CONTENTS

INTRODUCTION

According to legend, Ulysses was the founder of Lisbon. In fact it is not too far-fetched to think that the hero of the Odyssey might have decided to found a port not far from Cabo da Roca, the westernmost extremity of Europe: it would be just his style.

Legend apart, Lisbon is a modern capital, which has been shaped by a glorious and inspiring history, that of the great Discoveries, the period when heroic navigators in unlikely vessels, caravels, thought nothing of sailing off into the unknown and braving its thousands of real or imaginary dangers, in the 15C. Geographical knowledge quickly combined legends inherited from the past with scientific knowledge, without it always being possible to separate the two.

All this is here in the Lisbon of today, and those living in the city carry within them a pride in this history, which it claims as its own. And the city, although its face is turned to the future, is steeped in the past: in its architecture, with its Moorish influences, and its Manueline art, which could have been created only by a nation of sailors; in its topography; in the exuberance of its tropical gardens; in its undoubtedly Atlantic salt air; and in its civilization.

Lisbon is a paradox. Few capital cities are so Mediterranean, but here the Mediterranean is a long way away. More than that, it was Lisbon's port which, opening onto the vast Atlantic Ocean, brought about the irrecoverable economic and political decline of the Mediterranean. Lisbon is a good town for a stroll: up and down the steep lanes of Alfama, past teetering yellow trams which seem to have escaped from some transport museum, or through the lanes of the Bairro Alto, where you can sit down outside a café to take a small glass of *ginginha*, the cherry brandy of which the locals are so fond.

This is Lisbon – the explorers' town which in turn cries out to be explored. You can do this from the various viewpoints (*miradouros*) on its hills, but also by strolling around, by going into its *tascas*, by mixing with the people of Lisbon, and knowing how to listen. Lisbon will then open itself to you, and you might be changed by the experience.

Staggering, puffing, groaning, scraping the walls and parked cars, sometimes loaded down with a bunch of illegal passengers, it almost gives up the ghost...but no! Valiantly, the eléctrico tram manages to climb the steepest slopes!

BACKGROUND

GEOGRAPHY

The city of Lisbon is located approximately halfway between the north and the south of Portugal on the estuary of the **Tagus** (Tejo), a river more than 800km (500 miles) long. It rises in Spain in the mountains of Cuenca, and its estuary forms an incomparable natural harbour opening onto the Atlantic, the only large-capacity harbour which the country offers.

View across the rooftops of Lisbon from Castelo de São Jorge, with the 25 April Bridge spanning the Tagus in the background.

The town is the capital of a region called **Estremadura** (The Border). It was once the southern boundary of the territories reconquered from the Moors. Estremadura, which is now home to one-third of all Portuguese people, is a rich and fertile region famous for its magnificent coastal pine forests. Eucalyptuses, cereals, olive trees, vines and fruit trees are cultivated. Cliffs and long sandy beaches, which enjoy a very sunny climate, alternate along the coast.

But it is the Tagus, with its vast 'inland sea', the **Mar de Palha** (Straw Sea), so called because of the golden colour of its waters, which made Lisbon's fortune and shaped its destiny. This vast estuary (14km/8.7 miles wide) then shrinks to form a narrow channel which is dominated by the Tower of Belém, before opening onto the Atlantic Ocean. It is crossed by the **25 April Bridge**, the largest suspension bridge in Europe, which is high enough to allow the largest vessels to gain access to the Straw Sea.

The city proper is built on the northern side of the estuary. Like all Roman cities, it is proud to have Seven Hills (Estrela, Santa Catarina, São Pedro de Alcântara, São Jorge, Graça, Senhora do Monte and Penha de Franca), although there seem to be a good dozen. These hills provide a backdrop to the lower town, or Baixa, the 18C town and, further to the east, the modern city.

With its ever-busy port, with shipyards and an oil terminal, Lisbon is also the main industrial centre of the country (steel works, food processing works, cement works), and business districts have grown up at Campo Pequeno and Campo Grande, not far from the airport.

HISTORY

Birth of a Nation

Although archaeological research appears to show that the site of Lisbon was occupied in the Neolithic period, the foundation of the city is normally regarded as going back to the **Phoenicians**, who established a port there known as **Alis Ubo**, 'the calm roadstead', around 1200 BC. It is this name which, frequently distorted, has persisted right through to the present. The port, which became Olisipo, was then occupied by the **Greeks** and the **Carthaginians**, before the arrival of the **Romans**, who took it over in 205 BC, baptising it Felicitas Julia, and making it the capital of the province of Lusitania.

After the fall of the Empire, the town passed into the hands of the **Suebi** (407) and then the **Visigoths** (585), but lost its importance. The **Moors**, who landed in Spain in 711, took Lisbon in 714, fortifying it and baptising it Lissabona. The town was then subject to the Emirate of Cordoba, and experienced a period of economic and cultural prosperity. It was under the Moorish domination that the city, essentially the area around the present Castelo de São Jorge (the districts of Alfama and Mouraria), was divided into specialist quarters (residential areas, workshops, markets) and that the blue tiles, *azulejos*, were introduced via Spain.

Nevertheless, the **Christian reconquest** of the Iberian peninsula was beginning, led by the fighting monks of the Hospitallers and Templars under the patronage of **Alfonso VI**, the king of Léon and Castille. His daughter, the wife of Henry of Burgundy, gave birth to **Afonso Henriques**, who, from

An illuminated manuscript depicting the genealogical tree of Afonso Henriques who proclaimed himself first King of Portugal in 1139. Around the tree are paintings of his victories and an early panorama of Lisbon.

being merely count of Portugal, proclaimed himself king, and confirmed the independence of the country before retaking Lisbon from the Arabs on 25 October 1147. In 1255 his successor, **Afonso III** transferred the capital of the now entirely reconquered kingdom, with the frontiers which it still has today, from Coimbra to Lisbon. Lisbon benefited from its geographical position, halfway by sea between Holland and Italy, to profit from the commercial exchanges which developed between the cities in these two countries. In particular, many Genoese merchants set up in the town, which began to expand beyond its fortifications.

Navigators and Discoveries

The uncle of Afonso V, **Henry the Navigator** (1394-1460), is regarded as being responsible for Portugal's colonial vocation. After taking part in the expedition of 1415, which gave the fleet control of the Straits of Gibraltar (the key to the riches of the Sudan: gold and slaves), Prince Henry surrounded himself with astronomers, map makers and sailors to seek a direct sea route between Europe and the Indies, as the spice and perfume trade was then still in the hands of the Moors who controlled the land routes. These were the members of the school at Sagres, who replaced medieval cogs with caravels, an innovation which made the great Discoveries possible. The contribution of these light craft, which could sail into the wind, was invaluable. Technical progress in shipbuilding, and the invention of navigation instruments such as the astrolabe, allowed expeditions to push back the frontiers of the known world.

Henry the Navigator is widely credited as the architect behind Portugal's colonial expansion in the 15C.

Madeira was colonised in 1419, the Azores in 1427. In 1434 Cape Bojador, in the south of Morocco, was rounded, and Portugal obtained from the Pope a monopoly for trade with and the establishment of trading stations in Africa. Rather than conquer territories, the Portuguese preferred to establish trading stations (*feitorias*) on the coast, or trading companies. The mouth of the Congo was reached in 1482, and in 1488 **Bartolomeu Dias** rounded the Cape of Storms (which João II rebaptised the 'Cape of Good Hope'), the southernmost point of Africa.

Nevertheless, despite his interest in

It was João II who rejected Columbus's expedition to the Indies via a Western route.

navigation, **João II**, who ascended the throne in 1481, rejected the proposal by a Genoese navigator, Christopher Columbus, to attempt to reach the Indies by the Western route. Thus the New World was discovered for the Catholic kings of Castille in 1492. But with a bull from the Pope Alexander Borgia, through the **Treaty of Tordesillas** (1494), he achieved a share of the lands which were to be discovered: to the west of a meridian drawn 370 sea leagues from the Cape Verde islands, the lands would belong to Castille; to the east they would belong to Portugal. It was this which made it possible for Portugal to colonise Brazil

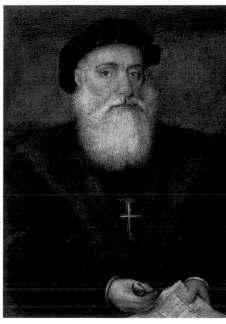

The great explorer Vasco da Gama discovered a sea route to India via the Cape of Good Hope in 1498.

(which was undiscovered at the time).

In 1497 **Vasco da Gama** embarked, with the aim of reaching the Indies by rounding the Cape of Good Hope. After a stop in Mozambique (March 1498), Vasco da Gama reached Calicut on 20 May. The sea route to the Indies was then opened, while in 1500 **Pedro Álvares Cabral** discovered Brazil. The governor, **Albuquerque**, set up trading stations and forts at strategic locations such as Goa, Ormuz and Macao. It was another Portuguese, **Magalhães** (Magellan), who achieved Columbus's dream of reaching the Indies by travelling westwards. In 1522 one of the vessels of his fleet returned to port after circumnavigating the world for the first time. However, this was for the benefit of the King of Spain, Charles V.

These Discoveries had a profound influence on the development of the world in the early 16C. The monopoly on trade with the Indies, which had previously been held by the Arabs and the Turks, passed into the hands of Portugal. The Mediterranean lost its primacy in international trade, which led to the decline of cities like Genoa and Venice, to the benefit of the Atlantic ports and, primarily, Lisbon, which became the hub of the European economy. African and Brazilian gold, spices from the Indies, silks from China, carpets from Persia, precious metals from Sumatra – such were the products which the city could offer, in exchange for arms, cereals, silver and copper.

Lisbon benefited from this prosperity. Between 1530 and 1630 the number of inhabitants increased from 65 000 to 160 000. The port sheltered more than 3 000 ships. The city grew along the Tagus towards the west (the Bairro Alto) and became adorned with monuments such as the Jerónimos Monastery and the Tower of Belém, which are decorated in the exuberant style of maritime inspiration to which **Manuel I** lent his name: **Manueline art**.

This was a period of cultural flowering linked with the name of **Camões** (1525-1580), the author of the famous *Lusiades* (1572), an epic glorifying the Portuguese explorers, in particular, Vasco da Gama.

But economic difficulties soon arose, and the catastrophic North African campaign of **Sebastião I**, killed in Morocco on 4 August 1578 during the **Battle of the Three Kings**, plunged the country into chaos. The Spanish profited from this, by taking over Lisbon and proclaiming **Philip II** king of Portugal in 1582. It was not till the rising, led by Duke João of Bragança (who proclaimed himself king under the name of **João IV**, in 1640) that Portugal recovered its independence. The new dynasty of the Braganças reigned until 1910.

Disaster and Enlightenment

Under the **House of Bragança**, and following the signature of a treaty with England in 1703 (the English immediately acquired a monopoly over the wine trade), the colonisation of Brazil led to unprecedented (although precarious) prosperity, which was reflected in the building of the **Águas Livres** (Free Water) aqueduct, 58km (36 miles) long, which still supplies Lisbon with water.

On 1 November 1755, a terrible **earthquake** devastated Lisbon while many of the inhabitants were attending All Souls' Mass. The palaces, churches and houses in the centre of the town were destroyed, and the candles from the churches spread fires throughout the city. In panic, the inhabitants of Lisbon who had survived dashed towards the Tagus, only to be confronted by an enormous tidal wave, sweeping away everything before it and destroying the lower town. This disaster resulted in an incalculable number of victims (sources say between 10 000 and 50 000), and sank its fortunes.

A new Lisbon was born under the enlightened leadership of the minister Sebastião José de Carvalho e Melo, better known as **Marquis de Pombal**. A kindred spirit of the luminaries, keen on modernising the country and developing education, and of an anticlerical bent (he expelled the Jesuits), Pombal transformed this disaster into his major work. After levelling the ruins of the Baixa (the lower town) he undertook its reconstruction on a rational and functional plan, adopting the designs of the architect Manuel da Maia – broad perpendicular avenues, relatively plain identical buildings, and activities grouped by areas, creating the lower town which can be seen today.

Manueline Art

What has been known since the 19C as Manueline art (also 'the architecture of the sea' or the 'Atlantic style') is an architectural style marking the transition between flamboyant Gothic and the Renaissance, which appeared in the reign of **Manuel I**, between 1490 and 1520. This original style reflects the confidence of the Portuguese, then at the peak of the commercial power brought by the Discoveries and their trading stations, and their passion for the sea and navigation.

More than simply an architectural style, its innovation lies in the element of decoration and in the movement of spirally twisting columns. The buildings of this time remain Gothic in plan, but they are covered with exuberant sculptures. Windows, doors, rose windows and balustrades are embellished with plant motifs such as laurel leaves, roses or maize stalks, or, more commonly, sculptures inspired by the sea (ropes, knots, anchors, marine creatures, etc.). Also characteristic are dynastic emblems: coats of arms; armillary spheres (a globe consisting of circles symbolising the tracks of the stars) designed to exalt the power of Dom Manuel; and the Cross of the Order of Christ, a religious and military order which helped to finance the Voyages of Discovery.

Although the Manueline style is found in several monuments in Portugal (such as the Monastery of Batalha, by Mateus Fernandes, and the

famous window at Tomar, the work of Diogo de Arruda), it is in the Belém area of Lisbon that Manueline art achieved its most successful expression in the **Jerónimos Monastery★★★** and, opposite this, at the edge of the Tagus, the **Tower of Belém★★★**.

It was an artist of French origin, **Boytac**, who directed the building of the Jerónimos Monastery in its initial years, between 1502 and 1517. The south portal, with its twisted columns surmounted by spiral pinnacles framed by two marvellously decorated windows, is regarded as his masterpiece, but the cloister embellished with nautical and exotic parrot motifs is also a magnificent example of the Manueline style. **Francisco de Arruda**, the architect of the Tower, introduced motifs of Moorish inspiration such as the horseshoe arch.

The cloisters of Jerónimos Monastery are a superb example of the Manueline style.

Searching for Stability

The ally of England, Portugal was a member of the coalition set up by the former against republican France in 1793. In 1807 the country was called upon by Napoleon I to take part in the continental blockade against its main trading partner, England. When this was refused, three French expeditions were sent, led by Junot (1807), Soult (1809) and Masséna (1810), but these could not penetrate the lines of defence of the English troops under the future Duke of Wellington. Portugal found itself the theatre of operations in a war which spread beyond its frontiers, and the effects on its political and economic well-being and on its people's morale were profound indeed. The Royal Family was exiled to Brazil in 1808 and Lisbon lost its role as capital city, to the benefit of Rio de Janeiro. It only regained it in 1823, with the return of **João VI**.

The 19C and early 20C were marked by the English occupation, many political upsets, sometimes bordering on civil war, and the independence of Brazil in 1822. An impoverished economy (the kingdom declared itself bankrupt in 1892) did not help matters, even though Portugal then set up its third empire in Angola and Mozambique. After a period of dictatorship, **Carlos I** and the crown prince were assassinated in Lisbon (Praça do Comércio) on 1 February 1908. The younger son, **Manuel II**, who had escaped the attempt, acceded to the throne but a republican landslide in the elections and a military rising forced him to abdicate on 5 October 1910 and leave the country.

The Republic did not succeed in restoring the situation and a *coup d'état* resulted in a dictatorship in 1926. Two years later, General Carmona called upon a professor of political economy at the University de Coimbra, **António de Oliveira Salazar** (1889-1970), to re-establish the economy. Becoming Prime Minister in 1932, Salazar built the **Estado Novo** (New State) over a period of 50 years, a particularly authoritarian regime marked by a very austere monetarist policy, to the detriment of economic growth.

The post-war period saw a massive emigration of Portuguese to industrial Europe, which did little to help the economic situation. The start of the Angolan revolt (1961), in which the Portuguese army became enmeshed in a war which was to last more than ten years, was a further drain on Portugal's resources and fuelled the increasing antagonism towards the regime.

Praça Luís de Camões was one of the sites where the people of Lisbon ignored orders to stay at home during the Carnation Revolution.

From Carnations to the Year 2000

It was the Armed Forces, led by **General Spínola**, which overturned the regime. On 25 April 1974, at half-past midnight, the *coup d'état* succeeded, without encountering any resistance. Despite appeals made on the radio, the population invaded the Praça do Comércio and cheered the soldiers, placing red carnations in the muzzles of their rifles in celebration of what became known as the **Carnation Revolution**.

After a disturbed period, Portugal found the way to stability with a democratic regime. The last colonies obtained their independence in 1975. Lisbon entered the EEC on 1 January 1986. Today, after having celebrated its glorious past during Expo 98, dedicated to the themes of the Ocean and Discovery, Portugal, strengthened by an economic growth amongst the most buoyant in Europe, is preparing for the challenges of the 21C by taking over the Presidency of the EU for the first six months of the year 2000.

PEOPLE AND CULTURE

There is a very apposite saying that the Portuguese 'live through their dreams and survive on salt cod'. Perhaps this should be seen as a key to the Portuguese character – lively and bright, ready to drop everything to go off and discover another world, but at the same time hardworking and tied to their soil, with a levity yet also sometimes seized with melancholy, the famous *'saudade'* (nostalgia) from which *fado* draws its inspiration.

The Portuguese are welcoming and are particularly proud to help you discover their country. Those of you who have Portuguese friends or colleagues will often have experienced this. For others, there is nothing easier than making contact in the *tascas*, those popular eateries where friends are quickly made and where the cooking, although simple, is often of high quality.

Between Dream and National Pride: Sebastianism

The national defeat of the Crusade undertaken in 1578 by the young king, Dom

Sebastião, who wanted to Christianise North Africa, ended as a double disaster: the **Battle of the Three Kings**, in which the sovereign and 8 000 of his soldiers were killed, and the loss of national sovereignty, because Spain took advantage of the defeat to annex the kingdom of Portugal.

Yet it was from these disasters that a new movement was born, 'Sebastianism'. It was based on the legend that Dom Sebastião was not dead, and would one day come back to drive out the invader. Apart from the sometimes bizarre aspects attendant upon this belief, Sebastianism became a symbol of national pride, felt all the more keenly as the vagaries of history and the uncertainties of the economy have led many Portuguese to live outside the frontiers of their country.

It is estimated that approximately one-third of Portuguese live abroad. There has been much emigration from Portugal over the last two centuries: to Brazil, Argentina and Venezuela in the 19C, to Angola and

The Portuguese people's lively enjoyment of shopping and bargain-hunting is best experienced at one of the many street markets such as this one in Alfama.

Mozambique in the early 20C, and more recently to Northern Europe. It is estimated that 1.5 million left the country between 1960 and 1972. But despite distance, traditions and attachment to the home country have been maintained, and there are few who do not return home when they can, for public holidays or for retirement.

Lively Traditions...

It is said that the people of Lisbon live together and live out of doors. Shops are, above all, somewhere to meet and exchange the latest gossip. The streets are cluttered with newspaper kiosks (reading newspapers is a national pastime in Portugal, which is practised daily in public parks, outside cafés or on public benches), and are the home of lottery ticket sellers, hawkers and shoeblacks. Cheap restaurants are packed, and people prefer to watch football matches on public televisions in cafés rather than in the solitude of their own flats.

The beach at Cascais is a popular weekend retreat from the city.

Traditions and lifestyle are transmitted from generation to generation partly through the strength of family values, but also because of the important role of grandparents in the education of young children.

It is in this way that traditions are perpetuated, like the religious festivals in the month of June (often somewhat pagan, a reminder of the summer solstice celebrations). Organised at midnight in the working-class districts of Lisbon, they celebrate the memory of a scion of the country, Fernando Bulhões, who is better known by the name of St Anthony of Padua. People gather in the streets, which are decorated with fairylights and garlands; they organise *sardinhadas*, followed by dancing and fireworks, and children sell bread rolls, the *paezinhos* of Santo António, while awaiting the official processions (*marchas populares*) organised on the Praça do Comercio. Also, as a reminder of the pagan cult of the dead, there is the tradition of illuminating family graves on 2 November.

... in a Modern Country

Yet the style of life is similar to that in all Western capitals. Weekends see a massive exodus to the beaches, both those of the *linha* (served by the railway line which runs along the shore as far as Cascais) and those of the Costa da Caparica, on the other side of the Tagus. Crossing the 25 April Bridge in a car on a Sunday night, bound for Lisbon, can be quite tedious. As for the young, their lifestyle, their clothes and their musical tastes are no different from those of their contemporaries in other European countries.

MUST SEE

Belém★★

The district fromwhere the caravels (light, fast ships) used to embark to discover unknown lands: from the symbolic **Torre de Belém★★**, situated on the Tagus, to the Manueline splendour of the **Mosteiro dos Jerónimos★★★**; from the ships in the **Museu da Marinha★★** to the furniture in the **Museu do Design★**, housed in the impressive **Centro Cultural★** – all tastes are catered for.

Museu Gulbenkian★★★ (Gulbenkian Museum)

In a garden of dreams, nestle outstanding collections, assembled by the Gulbenkian Foundation.

Museu Nacional de Arte Antiga★★★ (Museum of Ancient Art)

An extraordinary **Japanese screen** and a superb **polyptych** by Nuno Gonçalves are the masterpieces of this museum, located in the 17C Palace of the Counts of Alvor.

Alfama★★

Enjoy a pleasant stroll through timeless Lisbon which sings the *fado*: with its *miradouros*, narrow lanes along which the trams jangle, and alleys punctuated by stairways. Visit the **Sé★** (Cathedral) at the foot of the hill or, right at the top, the **Castelo de São Jorge★★**, from where there is a panoramic **view★★** over the city and river.

Baixa★★

Product of the Age of Enlightenment, this new 18C town was built on a grid plan. Beyond the **Praça do Comércio★★** it opens onto the Tagus.

Madre de Deus★★

The Baroque monastic buildings and **church★★** house the spectacular **Museu Nacional do Azulejo★★** (National Museum of Azulejos), dedicated to the emblem art of Portugal – a must for any visitor!

Palácio dos Marquêses de Fronteira★★
(Palace of the Marquises of Fronteira)
The palace, surrounded by superb gardens, is decorated with lovely **azulejos★★** illustrating both humorous and rustic scenes.

Sintra★★★

A charming town at the foot of a lush *serra*: museums (of **modern art★** and **toys★**), parks, fountains and *quintas* surround the **Palácio Real★★**, whilst towering on the mountain is the extraordinary **Palácio Nacional da Pena★★**.

The magnificent west portal of the Jerónimos Monastery.

THE TAGUS

Before entering the Atlantic through a
broad channel, the Tagus forms a small
inland sea which is known as the **Straw Sea**,
because of its golden reflections. The site of
the city is best appreciated by taking (like
the navigators of the past, but more
comfortably) a **river cruise★** (*cruzeiro no
Tejo*).

The boats follow the coast from the
Terreiro do Paço landing stage. In the
foreground lies the 18C town: the **Praça do
Comércio★★** opens onto the river and the
straight streets of **Baixa★★**. Then, after the
Chiado★ shopping centre and the popular
Bairro Alto★ district, the residential suburbs

*Crossing the Tagus
by ferry with the
elegant buildings of
Praça do Comércio
to the left.*

of **Lapa**, **Alcântara** and finally **Belém**★★ (AQ) conjure up the era of the Discoveries in the 16C. On the return trip, you travel along the left bank of the river where you discover the old district of **Alfama**★★, dominated by the cupola of the **Panteão Nacional**, the walls of the **Castelo São Jorge**★★ and the massive towers of the **Sé**★★ (cathedral).

Another way of navigating in Lisbon is to cross the estuary on board a regular ferry (*cacilheiros*), which depart from the Estaçao do Sul e Sueste or from the Cais do Sodre.

Port of Lisbon

Lisbon remains an important port of call in Europe. Wharves, warehouses (wine stores, oil facilities, refrigerated plants for the storage of cod, cork processing, etc.) and maritime terminals line the banks and, more particularly, on the Outra Banda (the other bank), where oil tankers and cargo ships moor close to the industrial zone.

Fashionable bars and discos occupy the old docks between the Tagus and the Avenida 24 Julho, and on Friday and Saturday nights are frequented well into the early hours by the young of Lisbon.

Ponte 25 de Abril★ (25 April Bridge)

Before 1966 there was no bridge in Lisbon, and the Tagus could be crossed only by boat or ferry. Building the **25 April Bridge**★ (BQ) took four years. It is the longest suspension bridge in Europe, spanning almost 2.3km (1.5 miles) and standing 70m (230ft) above the water (*toll on the left bank*). The **view**★★ when driving towards Lisbon is superb. Below the roadway deck, a railway line connecting Lisbon with the suburbs to the south was opened in July 1999.

Cristo Rei

By car, 3.5km (2 miles) from the toll on the 25 April Bridge. Take the second motorway exit on the left and follow the 'Cristo Rei' signs. By ferry, access in 10 minutes from Praça do Comércio to Cacilhas, where a No 9 bus will take you to the site. Open from 9am-6pm; 7pm in July/August.

This giant statue – a smaller replica of Christ the Redeemer in Rio de Janeiro – was inaugurated on 17 May 1959 to thank God for having spared Portugal during the Second World War. The pedestal (accessed by a lift, followed by 74 narrow stairs) is 85m (279ft) above the ground and 113m (371ft) above the Tagus, and supports the 28m (92ft) statue of **Christ the King**. A splendid **view★★** takes in the estuary, the city and the plain to the south.

The towering statue of Cristo Rei looks out across the Tagus.

Parque das Nações★ (Park of the Nations)

This is the name given to the area where Expo 98 took place (DN). The exhibition celebrated the discovery of the sea route to India by Vasco da Gama, and provided an opportunity to develop an industrial site to the east of Lisbon, alongside the Tagus, which had been neglected up until then. It was the first large-scale operation to modify the face of part of the city since the 18C construction of the Baixa by Pombal.

Take the Oriente underground and experience the boldly innovative **Estação do Oriente★**, a railway station covered by an amazing structure of glass and steel. An immense shopping centre, the **Centro Vasco da Gama**, provides access to the park itself, with its contemporary sculptures, fountains, restaurants, cafés and scattered exhibition buildings. Some have been converted to house fairs, while the Council of Ministers meets in the former **Pavilhão de Portugal** (designed by Álvaro Siza Vieira). The **Pavilhão Multiusos** (designed by Regino Cruz), a huge, egg-shaped building, is used for concerts and sporting events.

Start at the **Torre Vasco da Gama**, whose 104m- (340ft-) long terrace provides wonderful views over the Straw Sea. You may wish to seize the opportunity to have lunch at the *Restaurante Panorémico* ☎ 21 893 9550. Then on to explore the leisure park much appreciated by the inhabitants of Lisbon, by taking the **Teleférico** which overlooks the river, or by walking along the river on the **Passeio das Tágides**. In the distance, to the north, the 18km- (11 mile) long **ponte Vasco da Gama★★** stands out across the Tagus estuary. This is the most spectacular achievement in this new urban district.

Expo 98 is over... but Gil, its mascot, is still here to welcome visitors, young and old, to its Parque das Nações!

On your way, discover the exotic gardens, **Garcia de Orta**, the **Água Gardens**, and the **Oceanário★★**. The latter, located on the Olivais *doca* (quay), is the largest aquarium in Europe. Four tanks, laid out around an enormous central tank, recreate the ecosystems of the Atlantic, Indian, Pacific and Arctic Oceans. More than 25 000 fish, aquatic birds and mammals are visible on two levels. Children (up to 12) are welcome in the **Parque infantil do Gil** but, for those who crave strong sensations, all kinds of 'extreme' experiences are on offer in the **Parque Adrenalina**!

Many of the 18C buildings which surround Praça do Comércio have cool, shaded arcades.

THE BAIXA★★

'This is the end of the world!' exclaimed Voltaire's Candide, amidst the ruins of the town devastated by the earthquake and subsequent tidal wave on 1 November 1755. But reconstruction work was underway quite quickly, based on the gridiron plan laid down by the Marquis of Pombal (which is why the Lower Town is called the Pombal Centre), one of the few men to keep his head when faced with this catastrophe.

An extended rectangle between two large squares (Rossio and Praça do Comércio) (KXYZ), this district of uniform buildings, in a classical style impeccably aligned along straight avenues, is now a hive of activity. The Baixa houses not only commercial and government offices, but also countless shops of all kinds, especially jewellery and pastries. During the day, there is constant activity in these partly pedestrianised streets, which often bear the names of the corporations which Pombal settled there.

Praça do Comércio★★
(Commerce Square)
Before the terrible earthquake, the Royal Palace stood facing the Straw Sea. The palace was completely demolished, but its memory lives on in the square's informal name, the **Terreiro do Paço** (Palace Terrace) (KZ). The square opens onto the

river, and it was here that in former times
spices and gold from the Portuguese empire
were unloaded.

Today, arcaded 18C buildings house
various ministries and the Stock Exchange.
At no 3 is a bicentenary building, *Martinho
das Arcadas*, where **Fernando Pessôa** wrote
part of his work. The central monument of
the famous square where, in 1908, King
Carlos I and his son were assassinated, is a
statue of José I. During rush hour Lisbon's
commuters bustle across the square to take
the ferries for the opposite bank from the
Sul e Sueste 'station', which is estensively
decorated with *azulejos*.

From the square, in season, you can take
the **eléctrico de turismo**, a 100-year-old tram
which tours the hills of Lisbon.

*The equestrian
statue of José I
stands in front of
the Arch of Victory.*

Arch of Victory

This 19C triumphal arch is the passageway
between the square and the major highway
to Baixa, the **Rua Augusta**, which is alive with
street pedlars and entertainers, and is lined
with shops, banks and fast food eateries.
This sector, partly pedestrianised, is laid out
in a grid pattern of streets, which bear very
evocative names, such as Rua dos
Douradores (Goldsmiths' Street), Rua dos
Sapateiros (Shoemakers' Street) and Rua da
Prata (Silver Street). In the 16C, the **Rua
Aurea** or Rua do Ouro (Gold Street) was the
centre for trade in this precious metal. It
remains a street of bankers and jewellers.

Núcleo Arqueológico da Rua dos Correeiros

*Guided tour (by appointment 48 hours in
advance ☎ 21 321 1700), Friday and Saturday.*
As in all towns where succeeding civilizations
have existed for thousands of years,

A colourful flower stall on the Rua Augusta.

excavation works sometimes bring pleasant surprises. This is what happened in 1991 when work being carried on in the basements of the Banco Comercial Português (KYZ P) revealed important remains from the Roman period. The site had been occupied in succession by a pottery factory, a cemetery and an area of activities linked with fishing (25 salting tanks were uncovered). It now has glass paving through which you can see the various archaeological strata and the system of piles placed beneath the foundations of Pombal's buildings to protect them against earthquakes.

Elevador de Santa Justa★ (Lift)

Access by ticket or tourist pass obtainable from the kiosks of the Carris company. There is one at the bottom of the lift.

This all-metal lift (KY), with its cast-iron tracery, looks more like a machine for visiting the moon. It was built in 1902 by Raoul Mesnier de Ponsard, an engineer influenced by Gustave Eiffel. From the platform there is a fine **view★** over the town (access to Chiado is currently closed, for security reasons).

Rossio★

It was here that in the old days the Inquisition held its *auto da fés*. The old square was remodelled by Pombal, and it is now the main square of Lisbon (KX), situated at the opposite end of the Baxia to Praça do Comércio.

Under the gaze of Pedro IV, King of Portugal and the first sovereign of Brazil, a crowd of flower-sellers, souvenir- and lottery-

The extraordinary Elevador de Santa Justa, which provides good views over the Baixa.

ticket sellers ply their trades among the hubbub. This square is edged on three sides by 18C and 19C buildings whose ground floors are occupied by cafés and small shops which have retained their charming early-20C decoration. On the remaining side of the square is the **Teatro Nacional Dona Maria II** (Queen Maria II National Theatre), built around 1840 on the site of the Inquisition Palace. The bustling atmosphere of the Rossio continues in the nearby **Praça da Figueira** (Fig Tree Square), where lovers of ice creams and cakes will enjoy the mecca of the **Confeitaria Nacional** (at no 188).

The fountains of Rossio in front of the neo-Classical Teatro Nacional Dona Maria II.

Estação do Rossio (Rossio Station)
Serves the towns of Sintra and Queluz.
The station **façade★** (KX) is in neo-Manueline style (1890), with large horseshoe openings.

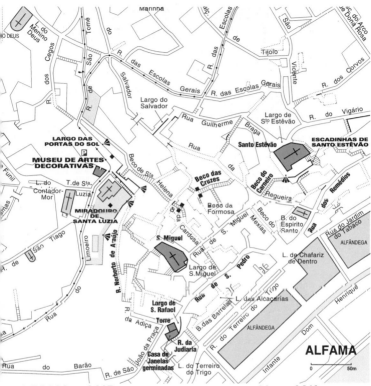

Map of Alfama

ALFAMA★★ AND THE MEDIEVAL TOWN★★

This district is best visited in the morning. It can be reached by tram No 28 to São Vicente de Fora, from where you can explore the district, returning by tram to the Baixa.

It is in this district which rises from the Tagus up the hill topped by Castelo de São Jorge, that Lisbon was born, and it is here that Lisbon's heart continues to beat.

The confusion of narrow streets, stairways and crowded buildings is typical of Alfama.

Alfama★★ (from the Arabic *alhama*, meaning hot water, a reference to the springs which burst out in the Largo das Alcaçarias) has been occupied since antiquity. It was here that the Visigoth town originally stood, and where later the Arabs built their palaces, followed by the Christians with their churches. Most of these early buildings were destroyed by the earthquake, the district was abandoned to sailors and fishermen and it took on its present appearance.

It is a confusion of often dilapidated (though sometimes renovated) buildings, with weather-beaten walls decorated with *azulejos* and wrought-iron balconies, housing superannuated shops, *fado* houses and the bars of the district, were you can stop to eat some grilled fish. The district is riddled with a maze of tortuous lanes and alleys (*becos*) punctuated by stairways and arches, giving the area an intimate village feel.

Yet despite the jumble of alleys, it is impossible to get lost. If you take the precaution of using one of the teetering and jangling yellow trams which seem to expend such efforts in getting up the hill, you then only have to follow the slope down and you will be back in the centre of town.

But do not go down too quickly. Spend a little time wandering around at random and you will find yourself in a place where the real Lisbon still survives, and where a surprise is to be found at every street corner – here the remains of an ancient Arab wall, there a Manueline doorway, next a fish market...

Igreja da São Vicente de Fora
Closed Mondays.

The church (MX) was built between 1582 and 1627 by Filippo Terzi. Its name 'de Fora', which means 'outside the walls', is a reminder of the fact that when it was built it lay outside the walls of Lisbon. A majestic stairway leads up to its fine façade.

In the cloisters to the south of the church, beautiful 18C **azulejos★** panels portray the fables of La Fontaine. Do not miss the

Looking down on the cloisters of Igreja da São Vicente de Fora, with their 18C azulejos panels.

cistern placed to collect rainwater. The
former refectory contains the coffins and
urns of kings and princes of the House of
Bragança.

Campo de Santa Clara★

This charming square behind São Vicente
de Fora church is surrounded by elegant
houses, and every Tuesday and Saturday is
the site of the **Feira da Ladra** (Thieves'
Market, *see* p.105), a colourful flea market
where there are bargains to be found among
the jumble and clothing. There is a fine view
of the Tagus from **Boto Machado Gardens**
(MX F).

Igreja de Santa Engrácia★

The church was begun in the 17C, but only
crowned with a dome and finally
consecrated in 1966. Thus the saying, 'Like
the work on Santa Engrácia' has passed into
the everyday language of Portugal, to mean
a job which is never finished.

The church is now the national
mausoleum (MX), containing the tombs of
leading lights of the Portuguese Discoveries,
such as Vasco da Gama, Henry the
Navigator, Cabral, Afonso de Albuquerque
and the poet Camões.

Castelo de São Jorge★★
(St George's Castle)
Open from 9am to sunset.
Perched on top of the hill, this 5C castle was
enlarged by the Moors in the 9C, then from
the 14C to the 16C was the residence of the
kings of Portugal.

Enter through the outer wall, which
encloses the **Santa Cruz District**, and you will
find yourself carried back to the Middle

St George's Castle provides magnificent
views across Lisbon.

Ages. From a vast esplanade (LY) shaded by pine, jacaranda and hackberry trees, there is a panoramic **view★★** over the city, the Tagus, the conurbations on the left bank, and the suspension bridge. Take in the view at leisure over lunch in the *Casa do Leao* restaurant (☎ 21 887 5962), or by visiting the **Olisipónia**, a multimedia walk through the history of Lisbon.

The nearby **Largo das Portas do Sol★** (Sun Gateway) was one of the seven gates of the Arab city. There is a very fine **view★★★** from the terrace.

Museu de Artes Decorativas★★
(Museum of Portuguese Decorative Arts)
In this 17C palace (LY M¹³), the Portuguese and Indo-Portuguese furniture, carpets, tapestries and goldsmiths' work provide the atmosphere of a fine 18C house with painted ceilings and *azulejos* panels. Among

Houses in the medieval quarter of Santa Cruz.

the finest objects in the museum are a travelling toilet set and a chess table. These collections were bequeathed to the city of Lisbon by the banker, Ricardo do Espírito Santo Silva. Today, they serve as models for the pupils of the School of Decorative Arts, housed by the Foundation.

Miradouro de Santa Luzia★ (Viewpoint)

Near Santa Luzia church, the viewpoint (LY L¹) is supported on the remains of ancient fortifications. From here, there is a very fine view over the Tagus and the roofs and lanes of the Alfama. The *azulejos* panels are interesting – they show the Praça do Comércio before the earthquake and the taking of Lisbon by the Crusaders.

The viewpoint of Miradouro de Santa Luzia looks out across the Tagus.

Stairways lead down to the Rua São Pedro

(where the fish market is held every morning) and the Rua dos Remédios, the most commercial roads in the Alfama, lined with small shops and taverns.

There are many viewpoints (*miradouros*) in Lisbon, and some have the added bonus of a café or bar to compliment the continually changing panorama. The **Miradouro da Senhora do Monte** offers a view over the entire centre, while the **Miradouro da Graça**, like the Miradora de Santa Luzia, also has a café. These provide the opportunity for a welcome halt – wandering around these steep streets can be hard work... especially in summer.

Casa do Fado e da Guitarra Portuguesa* (Museum of Fado and the Portuguese Guitar)

Located on the Largo de Chavariz de Dentro (MY), at the foot of the Alfama, the newest addition to Lisbon's museums provides an evocative walk through the history of the *fado*, and the very special Portuguese guitar. Documents, dioramas and reconstructions portray all aspects of the *fado*, whilst headphones allow you to listen to the great *fado* singers of yesterday and today. All in all, a welcome initiation before scouring the town in search of *fado* clubs!

Sé Patriarcal* (Cathedral)

Lisbon's cathedral served as a fortress in the Middle Ages, as witnessed by its fronting towers and the crenellated tops of its walls. Built in the 12C in a very severe Romanesque style, it was partly destroyed during the 1755 earthquake, which explains the composite style of the choir.

The **treasury★** (*closed on Sundays and public holidays*) houses magnificent ancient priests' vestments, with stunning embroidery work. Among the gold and silver plate is an extraordinary monstrance decorated with more than 4 000 precious stones. In the Gothic-style **cloisters** archaeological diggings uncovered traces of former dwellings, inlcuding the foundations of a mosque.

Not far away, in the Beco das Cruzes, is the site where Anthony of Padua (who, like many of his compatriots, gained glory by

The Cathedral's Gothic-style 13C cloisters afford a cool retreat during warm summer days.

The upper part of Casa dos Bicos was destroyed in the earthquake of 1755 and has only recently been restored.

Blue and white or polychrome, amusing or serious, abstract or narrative, these azulejos bring the walls alive!

leaving his native country) was born. The little church of **Santo António da Sé** now stands on the site. There are representations of St Anthony, patron saint of Lisbon, in the small **Museu Antoniano**.

Casa dos Bicos
(House of Facets)

At the foot of the Sé, in the Rua dos Bacalhoeiros, this palace (LZ C¹) owes its name to its façade covered with stones carved into diamond points. It belonged to the descendants of Alburquerque, the viceroy of India, who captured Goa in 1510.

Museu Nacional do Azulejo★★
(National Museum of Azulejos)

To the east of the centre of town, in Rua da Madre de Deus. Access from Praça do Comércio by bus 104. Closed on Mondays.

The museum, which has been set up in the buildings of the **Madre de Deus** (Mother of God) Convent (DP M¹⁷), illustrates the process of manufacturing tile panels, and traces their development. The great **Nativity of Nossa Senhora da Vida** (1580) is a very fine example of Italian influence over the first *azulejos* manufactured in Portugal.

The delightful small Manueline cloister is decorated with its original *azulejos* (16C-17C), and the stairway is bordered by sumptuously framed panels. On the upper floor, 18C blue and white panels illustrate battles or scenes from daily life – notice the doctor giving an injection, the amusing leopard hunt and the panoramic view of Lisbon before the earthquake. The final rooms show that the art of *azulejos* is far from dead, and includes works by contemporary artists like Julio Pomar and Vieira da Silva.

The **Madre de Deus★★** church (DP) (*closed at present for major renovations*) was rebuilt at the end of the 18C after the earthquake. The Baroque nave is spanned by a vault of gilded panels, while the lower parts of the walls are decorated with 18C Dutch tiles.

The gilded Rococo altar and sumptuous panels of Madre de Deus were added in the late 18C.

Azulejos

The etymology of the word is debatable: *zuléija* is the Arab word for a smooth piece of earthenware, while *azul* means blue. But whatever the exact derivation, it is indication enough that it was the Moors who introduced *azulejos* into the Iberian peninsula.

The first *azulejos* in Portugal were imported from Seville in the 15C. These brightly coloured tiles, used like a mosaic, were decorated with geometrical or plant designs. Very few survive today, except on the floor of the Chapel of Manuel I's Palace, **Sintra**.

From then on, *azulejos* became intimately linked with Portuguese architecture, and both their style and technique

Two fine examples from the National Museum of Azulejos.

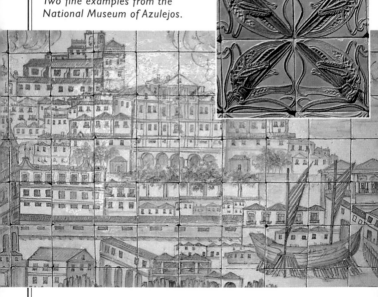

of manufacture has developed over the years.

It was during the 16C that the first *azulejos* influenced by the Italian *majolica* technique were made in Portugal. The decoration was applied to the tiles directly by brush, which made it possible to abandon geometrical designs for figurative representations. The influence of Flemish workers in ceramics led to the making of large polychrome panels, like those to be seen in **São Roque Church**★ (1584).

Under Spanish domination the decoration became more austere and the *tapetes* (tile-carpets) made their appearance. A basic geometric or floral design was reproduced and repeated in blocks of 4, 16 or 36 tiles, allowing church walls to be decorated inexpensively.

Figurative representation returned with the advent of the Bragança dynasty. Mythological scenes, caricatures and grotesques multiplied as colours developed. Copper green and manganese violet were added to the traditional yellows and blues. But this triumphant riot of colour gradually gave way to scenes painted in blue on a white background, influenced by Chinese porcelain and Delft pottery. The tableaux show people in idealised landscapes, battle scenes or edifying episodes from the lives of saints. The cloisters of **São Vicente de Fora** church illustrate this style.

The setting up of the Rato Royal Pottery Works in 1767 led to the rapid production in large quantities of the *azulejos* required, especially for the reconstruction of Lisbon.

In the 19C it was the fashion to cover house and shop fronts with glazed tiles, a trend thought to have been derived from Brazil where the tiles protected the walls against tropical rain and the humidity. Manufacture became semi-industrial, and patterns were printed and reproduced in large quantities.

Azulejos are still being produced in Portugal to decorate public buildings and, as a result of commissions from the State, Portuguese artists are going back to this hitherto somewhat neglected art form. The stations of the Lisbon underground are decorated with tiles created by painters such as Vieira da Silva, Júlio Pomar, Maria Keil and Eduardo Nery.

Conversation outside the shops of Rua Garrett.

THE CHIADO★ AND BAIRRO ALTO★

Twelve years after the fire which ravaged it on 25 August 1988, the **Chiado★** (KY) has come back to life. Reconstruction, in the hands of the Portuguese architect Álvaro Siza Vieira, has retained the original style. A lively shopping centre, **Armazem do Chiado**, has replaced the old department stores and the reconstructed buildings once again house fashion boutiques, fine bookshops (e.g. *Livraria Bertrand*) and pastry shops (e.g. *Bénard*). This is especially so in the **Rua do Carmo★**. The **Rua Garrett★**, which links the Rossio to Praça Luís de Camões, is a

A Poet by Any Name

Alvaro de Campos, Ricardo Reis, Alberto Caeiro – three Portuguese poets with very different styles. They never met, yet they shared one thing in common – they were some of the poets invented by **Fernando Pessõa** (1888-1935), a strange man of many personalities, who was passionate about Lisbon. Now, 65 years after his death, Pessõa, who published hardly anything under his real name and who made a living as a commercial translator on café terraces, is now recognised as one of the major contemporary poets. He left a considerable body of work which, too busy writing, he never took the time to publish, and stuffed into a trunk; it was opened 10 years after his death. He is regarded in Portugal as a symbol of the nation – to the extent that his ashes were transferred to the cloister of Jerónimos Monastery in Belém in 1985, to lie alongside those of Camões.

The seated statue of the poet Fernando Pessõa at the café A Brasileira.

One of his works, *Lisbon*, although written in 1925, will enable Pessõa enthusiasts to retrace his steps to the restaurant *Martinho das Arcadas* (Praça do Comercio) or visit him at the Casa Pessõa, near the Jardim da Estrela, now converted to a library and cultural centre.

meeting place for the young of Lisbon. Take a break from sightseeing on the terrace of the famous café **A Brasileira**, alongside the statue of the poet Fernando Pessõa. Or wander along the Rua Ivens, on your left, with its beautiful mansions, stopping at the **Café Rosso**, located in an inner courtyard (access at no 57), until you reach the Largo da Académia Nacional de Belas Artes where you will find one of the best restaurants in Lisbon, the **Tágide** (at no 18 ☎ 21 342 0720).

Praça Luís de Camões

This square has become one of Portugal's most important historic sites since the Carnation Revolution of 1974, which restored freedom to the country. It is one of the places where the people ignored the military's orders to stay home, but swarmed onto the street to join them in celebrating the end of 40 years of dictatorship.

The **Bairro Alto★** (JXY), the 17C residential district, can be reached on foot or by the funiculars (*elevador*) of Glória and Bica. It is now an artists' quarter, with galleries and craft boutiques. Popular for its *fado* night-spots, it has a reputation for its intellectual and

At night, on leaving the Tágide, suddenly glimpse through the gate of a private car park a view over the Baixa and Alfama, where the massive towers of the Sé are outlined in the dark. Magical!

Glória funicular in the Bairro Alto.

bohemian atmosphere, with many bars and restaurants to choose from. The main shopping streets are the Rua do Diário de Notícias and the Rua de Atalaia.

There is a fine view of the 25 April Bridge and the Tagus from the **miradouro do Alto de Santa Catarina★** (JYZ A¹). The giant on his pedestal here is Adamastor who, according to legend, was changed into the Cape of Storms (Cape of Good Hope).

Igreja do Carmo★ (Carmelite Church)
Passing through the church door, the eye is immediately drawn upwards to the sky, which can be seen through the fragments of the vaulted ceiling which collapsed in the earthquake on 1 November 1755. It is a strangely enchanting place, especially if you are lucky enough to attend an evening concert under a summer starry night. Alas, this is not possible at present, as building

Behind its shady entrance are the remains of the Carmelite church.

operations have made the site unstable and
the church (KY M⁴) is closed to the public.

Igreja de São Roque★ (Church of St Rock)
This Jesuit church (JX) was built at the end
of the 16C, though the original façade
collapsed during the great earthquake. The
interior★ is striking for its elegant decoration.
The painted wood ceiling of the nave shows
scenes from the Apocalypse. The third chapel
on the right has interesting 16C *azulejos*.

The **Capela de São João Baptista★★**
(Chapel of St John the Baptist) – fourth on
the left – ordered by João V, represents a
technical *tour de force*. It was designed and
built in Rome by some 130 artists, and
transported to Lisbon 'in kit form' by three
ships and re-erected around 1750. It is
exceptional for the richness of its materials:
columns of lapis lazuli, altar front of amethyst,

*The sumptuous
Chapel of St John
the Baptist is one of
the highlights of the
Church of St Rock.*

Details of an 18C priest's vestments, from the Museum of Sacred Art.

steps of porphyry, angels of Carrara marble and ivory and friezes, capitals and ceiling embellished with gold, silver and bronze.

Museu de Arte Sacra de São Roque★
(Museum of Sacred Art)

Closed Mondays. Next to Igreja de São Roque.
This small, modern museum (M¹¹) contains 16C Portuguese paintings and some of the treasure King João V ordered from Italian artists for the Chapel of St John the Baptist, in the 18C. The collection of **priests' vestments★**, made of silk and embellished in gold, is unique and a remarkable example of the skill of the embroiderers.

Miradouro São Pedro de Alcântara★
Opposite the **Solar do Vinho Porto** where port wines can be tasted (*Rua São Pedro de Alcântara 45; closed Sundays and public holidays; open evenings until 11pm*), this small garden forms a balcony above the lower town (JX L²), offering an extensive **view★★** over the Baixa, the Tagus and the hill opposite with Castelo de São Jorge.

Fado

In the beginning there was a mood, *saudade*, a disturbing mixture of nostalgia and spirit of adventure, a vaguely melancholic rending. The art of the *fadista* (singer) is to express that *saudade*, to enable the audience to identify with the emotions, the mood, to take on the *saudade* themselves.

The fact that the word *fado* also means 'destiny' is undoubtedly significant. What is known of its origins suggests that it was initially more of a dance, of African origin, imported from Brazil by sailors and danced in the drinking dens of the port. Apart from this, the now famous *morna* of Cape Verde, recently popularised by **Cesaria Evora**, is also a cousin of the *fado*. It is impossible to say which influenced the other. Others claim that the haunting tones of the *fado* expressed the nostalgia of sailors far from their homes for long months, or those at home lamenting their absence.

Fado appeared in Lisbon around 1820, with the singer **Maria Severa**, who is still remembered, and became immediately popular in all

The house of Maria Severa has become a 'shrine' to fado fans.

strata of society. *Fado* houses opened from around 1833, and the literary character of the impassioned *fadista*, going from house to house taking her melancholy with her, listening to *fado* and nursing a drink, was born in the late 19C.

Universally known through **Amália Rodrigues**, *fado* is often sung by a woman with a high-pitched voice, accompanied by players of the *guitarra*, a deep twelve-stringed guitar imported from England.

A visit to the legendary *fadistas* in the Alfama quarter at the **Casa do Fado e da Guitarra Portuguesa★** is a must – you should then be able to recognise the real *fadistas*!

Museu Nacional de Arte Antiga★★★
(Museum of Ancient Art)

Rua da Janelas Verdes 9. Closed on Mondays and public holidays. Not far from the Tagus, towards Belém, served by buses 27, 40, 49 and 60.

At the base of Lapa Hill, the outstanding painting, sculpture and decorative arts collections of the Museum of Ancient Art (BQ M[16]), ranging from the 12C to the 19C, reflect the history of Portugal. The works are by Portuguese or European artists who lived in or had close links with Portugal. Some works were confiscated from monasteries in 1833 when religious orders were suppressed.

The most interesting painting in the museum is undoubtedly the **Polyptych of the Adoration of St Vincent★★★** painted by Nuno Gonçalves, painter to Afonso V, between 1460 and 1470. The panels of this polyptych had disappeared but were discovered in the late 19C in the attics of the monastery of São Vicente de Fora. They provide a valuable document on Portuguese society at the time. Clustered around St Vincent, the patron saint of Portugal, is Henry the Navigator, with princes, prelates, knights, monks and sailors, representing

One of the panels from the Polyptych of the Adoration of St Vincent, showing Infante Fernão kneeling before St Vincent.

all levels of society. The remarkable technique, the flamboyance of the solid colours used and the arrangement of the figures filling the entire space make this a key work in the history of painting.

Among paintings from other European schools, a prominent work is the extraordinary **Temptation of St Antony★★★**, by Hieronymus Bosch, with its grotesque creatures and infernal setting. Also look for the delightful *Virgin and Child* by Hans Memling, *St Jerome* by Dürer, and the

A detail from one of the 16C Japanese screens housed in the Museum of Ancient Art.

Twelve Apostles★ by Zubarán.

Unique **Japanese screens★★** depict the arrival of the Portuguese on the island of Tanegaxima in 1543. Each screen consists of six hinged panels. As in a comic strip, the people are shown in successive scenes. It is amusing to see how the Japanese saw the Portuguese, emphasising their physical characteristics – the long noses, moustaches, and the dark skin of some of the sailors.

The Portuguese as seen by the Japanese – the former clearly a mystery...

The museum also contains a major collection of goldsmiths' work, the most valuable piece being the **monstrance** from the **Mosteiro de Belém** (1506) which was made with gold brought back from India by Vasco da Gama.

The new wing of the museum includes the **Chapel of the Convent of Santo Alberto★**, richly decorated with gilded woodwork and *azulejos*.

THE MANUELINE WEST: BELÉM★★

From Praça do Comércio, Belém is 6km (3.7 miles) to the west alongside the Tagus, and is served by the very modern tramway 15 and buses 28 and 43. Car parking is relatively easy. As the railway cuts the site in two, there are underpasses and a footbridge. The monuments and museums are closed on Mondays.

To the west of the capital, on the bank of the Tagus, this district (AQ) has close links with Portugal's maritime epics. It was from Belém (the shortened form of 'Bethlehem' in Portuguese) that the Portuguese vessels which were to roll back the boundaries of the known world set sail in the 15C, and was the home port of the caravels which travelled the oceans. It was in this part of

Lisbon that the architectural reflection of the spirit of the Discoveries, Manueline art, developed its full expression.

The area includes not only the Tower of Belém and the Jerónimos Monastery, both of which are famous landmarks in the city, but also major museums, a modern cultural centre, many restaurants and a famous cake shop, **Antiga Confeitaria de Belém** (Rua de Belém 84/8), which is famous for its small custard tarts, the *pastéis de nata*. One of Lisbon's institutions!

Mosteiro dos Jerónimos★★★
(Jerónimos Monastery)

It was in 1502 that Manuel I decided to build this monastery (AQ). In this early part of the 16C the ships of Vasco da Gama moored close to Belém, bringing riches and power. The architecture of the monastery, which was intended for the Hieronymite monks (St Jerome), was designed to reflect the splendour of Manuel's reign, and is an outstanding example of the Manueline style.

Begun in Gothic style by the architect Boytac, who was of French origin, it was subject to several influences in the course of its construction – Manueline, Plateresque and then Renaissance, with classical touches in the final elements dating from the end of the 16C.

To the left of the belltower, 19C buildings contain the Maritime Museum and the National Archaeological Museum.

Igreja Santa Maria★★★ (St Mary's Church)
This masterpiece of Manueline art is entered through the **southern portal**. The richness of its decoration – with gables,

pinnacles, and an abundance of statues in niches – provides an immediate measure of the originality of this art form, which spans the transition between Gothic and the Renaissance. A statue of Henry the Navigator adorns the central pillar and seems to welcome visitors.

Inside it is hard to know which is more surprising – the boldness of the magnificent **vaulting**★★ or the extreme slenderness of the columns of the nave. It is interesting to note

The graceful columns of St Mary's Church.

that it all survived the 1755 earthquake, a testament to the skill of its creator, João de Castilho.

The chancel contains many tombs, including those of Manuel I and João III and their queens. The tombs of Vasco da Gama and the poet Camões lie beneath the gallery, at the entrance to the building.

Claustro★★★ (Cloisters)

The cloisters, too, are stunning. Take your time exploring them, preferably in the late afternoon when the sun gives the stone a warm colour, emphasising the richness of the decoration. An enormous square, with sides 55m (180ft) long, the cloisters rise to a height of two storeys. The lower storey is the work of Boytac, while the upper was designed by João de Castilho.

Museu Nacional de Arquelogia
(National Archaeological Museum)
This is located in the 19C wing of the Jerónimos Monastery. In the main gallery the various stages of the history of Portugal, from its origins to the end of the Roman period, are illustrated by pottery, weapons, jewels, funerary monuments and so on.

The strange *Berrões* (granite sculptures representing boars) dating from the Iron Age, which are frequent in north-east Portugal, are worth looking for.

Padrão dos Descobrimentos
(Monument to the Discoveries)
Opposite the Jerónimos Monastery and overlooking the Tagus from its height of 52m (170ft), this symbolic monument pays double homage: firstly, to **Prince Henry the Navigator** – it was erected in 1960 by the

When the sun sheds a golden light on the finely chiselled stone, it is an enchanting place!

sculptor Leopoldo de Almeida to mark the
500th anniversary of the Prince's death –
and secondly, to all those who guided
Portugal on the way to the great Discoveries.
At the prow of the ship which the
monument represents, Henry the Navigator
shows the way, followed by a number of
Portuguese heroes. Look, on the right-hand
side, for Manuel I carrying an armillary
sphere and Camões holding extracts from
The Lusiades. From the top (*access by lift*)
there is an exceptional **view** over the Tagus
and the district of Belém.

*The striking
Monument to the
Discoveries, with
Henry the
Navigator at the
prow.*

One of the magnificent royal galliots in the Barge Hall of the Maritime Museum.

Museu da Marinha★★ (Maritime Museum)
The Monument to the Discoveries stands like an invitation to come and discover the Maritime Museum (AQ M⁷), which records five centuries of Portugal's maritime history. The museum is housed on the esplanade in the two buildings flanking the **Calouste Gulbenkian Planetarium**.

Passing through the main room, you can follow an evocative display of the times of the great Discoveries, tracing the maritime history of Portugal from the 15C to the 18C, including splendid models of sailing ships, caravels and frigates, ships' figureheads and various navigational instruments. The 19C and 20C display includes models of modern warships and submarines.

In the **Barge Hall** there are seven magnificent galliots, including a remarkable ceremonial barge decorated by the Frenchman, Pillement, for the future king João VI's wedding in 1785, providing a reminder of the pomp and refined taste of 18C festivals.

Also in this part of the museum is the seaplane 'Santa Cruz', which made the first crossing of the Southern Atlantic in 1922.

Centro Cultural de Belém★ and Museu do Design★ (Belém Cultural Centre and Museum of Design)

The **Cultural Centre★** (AQ), a vast composition, built in white limestone by Vittorio Gregotti and Manuel Salgado, is very imposing. Housing exhibition halls, auditoria and cafés (one, the *Quadrante*, is set on the terrace overlooking the Tagus), it is a highlight of Lisbon cultural life.

The modern façade of the Belém Cultural Centre.

It also houses the **Museu do Design★**, with works by great names (Frank O. Gehry, Starck, Garouste, Gaetano Pesce) and well-known classics such as the *Marilyn couch* (1971).

Torre de Belém★★★ (Tower of Belém)

Before the 1755 earthquake changed the course of the Tagus, this tower, built by Francisco de Arruda between 1515 and 1519, stood on top of the rock in the middle of the estuary, where it served as both lighthouse and watch-tower. Today it has become the emblem of the city.

The sides of the square tower are embellished with finely decorated balconies, turrets and statues. Note the typically

The Tower of Belém is one of the best examples of Manueline architecture.

The Coach Museum, in the Palace of Belém, is one of the finest of its kind in the world.

Manueline ropework decoration. Jutting out from the tower is an extensive platform, designed for artillery and protected by battlements which are decorated with shields of the Cross of the Order of Christ.

Museu Nacional dos Coches★★
(Coach Museum)

The **Palace of Belém** (M^{22}) is the official residence of the President of the Republic, Visiting this very rich collection of vehicles, look for the late 16C painted Berlin (four-wheeled carriage) which belonged to Philip II of Spain, and the three huge coaches in Italian Baroque style, built in Rome (1716) for Portugal's ambassador to Pope Clement XI, the Marquis of Fontes. After temporary exile at the Parque das Nações, the collections should be returned to the Palace menage in the year 2000.

The Art Deco façade of the Eden Theatre now houses a modern store.

MODERN LISBON

Praça dos Restauradores

An extension of Rossio, this square is dedicated to the men who led the revolt which, in 1640, enabled Portugal to regain its independence. The west side of the square is taken up by the Art Deco fronting of the old **Eden Teatro** (now the Virgin Megastore) and the **Palacio Foz**, with its fine salmon pink roughcast façade, which houses the Tourist Information Office. Opposite, at no 58 in the picturesque **Rua das Portas de Santo Antão**, is the **Casa do Alentejo**, whose Moorish patio and upstairs dance hall and dining rooms are well worth a visit.

The wide, tree-lined Avenida da Liberdade links the old part of the city with Parque Eduardo VII. At the northern end is the imposing monument of the Marquis of Pombal.

Avenida da Liberdade★

This wide avenue (JV), with its shady palm trees and with pavements covered with mosaics tracing out black and white patterns and dotted with statues, extends the street area set out by the Marquis of Pombal to the north by 1 500m (1 mile). Simply called the Avenue, it is lined with hotels, cinemas, fashion boutiques and airline companies.

Praça Marquês de Pombal

This is the nerve centre of Lisbon, where its major avenues converge. In the middle of this circular space is a column crowned by the statue of the Marquis of Pombal (CP), who seems to be walking his pet lion.

Parque Eduardo VII★

This elegant park crowns the Avenida da Liberdade (CP). From the top there is a magnificent **view★** over the lower town and the Tagus, framed by the hills of Castelo de São Jorge and the Bairro Alto. The **cool conservatory★** (*estufa fria*) protects countless exotic plants growing around fish-filled pools, from the heat of summer and the rigours of winter.

The modern districts around the park and beyond are subdivided by a grid of major avenues: Fontes Pereira de Melo, República, Roma, Berna, etc. The town continues to grow, overtaking and absorbing districts such as Restelo and Benfica. Commuter townships occupy the surrounding hills.

Looking across the lawns and box hedges of Parc Eduardo VII to the busy centre of Lisbon, with the Tagus in the distance.

The luxuriant conservatory in the park is filled with an exotic collection of plants and trees.

The Gulbenkian Foundation

Calouste Gulbenkian, of Armenian origin, was born in Istanbul in 1869 and died in the Aviz Hotel in Lisbon in 1955. A pioneer oil magnate and great businessman, he was a founder of the Compagnie Française des Pétroles. In 1928 when the Turkish Petroleum Company was split up, he received a 5% share of the profits, hence his nickname 'Mr 5%'. Immensely rich, he was both a lover of art and a generous man, in particular to the Armenian community.

He took up residence in Portugal during the Second World War, and shortly before his death set up the Foundation for charitable, artistic, educational and scientific purposes. This private institution includes the Gulbenkian Museum (CP), the Modern Art Centre, an orchestra, a ballet company, and a choir. It distributes many bursaries to students, finances research, organises exhibitions and has two branch offices in London and Paris.

An 18C marble statue of Diana by Houdon, in the Gulbenkian Museum.

The museum and its park, where art and nature mingle in an enchanting place – a favourite with both walkers and geese and ducks!

Museu Gulbenkian★★★
(Gulbenkian Museum)

Avenida da Berna 45. To the north of the town centre, accessible via the underground (Palhavâ) or by buses 16, 26, 31, 41, 46 and 56. Closed Mondays and public holidays.

Opened in 1965 and with renovations pending at the beginning of 2000, this museum (CP) is set in hilly botanical gardens, dotted with lakes and modern sculptures and crossed by an artificial river where geese and ducks frolic.

The **Oriental art** section contains ancient artefacts and Islamic pieces – sumptuous carpets (mainly Persian), ceramics, tile panels in vivid colours, costumes made of silk and mosque lamps – reminding us that Gulbenkian was born in Turkey. There is porcelain from China, together with large prints and lacquerwork from Japan.

The **European art** section is strong on French art of the 18C, but there are also other delights such as the delicate ivories from the Middle Ages. Luxurious French furniture by Cressent, Jacob, Riesener, Oeben, Garnier and Carlin and sumptuous gold and silver tableware by F-T Germain illustrate the perfection of decorative arts in the 18C.

The collections of French, English and Italian painting include the great names of the 18C and 19C: Hubert Robert, Turner, Guardi, Manet, Degas and Renoir, to name but a few. This section honours Flemish and Dutch painting of the 16C and 17C, including in particular Van der Weyden (*St Joseph*), Rembrandt (*Picture of an Old Man*),

Rubens (*Portrait of Hélène Fourment*) and an admirable *Annunciation* by Thierry Bouts.

Among the sculptures, the magnificent *Diana* in white marble, by Houdon should not be missed. Finally, there is a room reserved for the exceptional works by the decorator René Lalique (1860-1945), who was a personal friend of Gulbenkian.

Centro de Arte Moderna José de Azeredo Perdigão★ (CAM)
(Modern Art Centre)

This recent creation (1983), the work of the British architect, Sir Leslie Martin, blends with the vegetation to such an extent that you get the impression that nature and the building are one. It houses modern works of art by Portuguese artists dating from 1910 to the present: Vieira da Silva, Amadeo Souza-Cardoso, Almada Negreiros and Julio Pomar.

A sculpture by Henry Moore outside the Modern Art Centre.

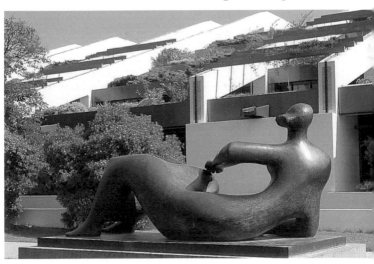

The Palace and gardens are influenced by the Italian Renaissance.

Palácio dos Marquêses de Fronteira★★
(Palace of the Marquises of Fronteira)
By underground to Sete Rios station, then a 20-minute walk through Rua das Furnas, over the railway footbridge and the largo São Domingos de Benfica. Guided visits from June to September, every half hour from 10.30am to noon, and from October to May at 11am and noon. Closed on Sundays and public holidays.

The palace, located to the north of **Parque Florestal de Monsanto★** (Monsanto Park) (ABP), was built around 1670 by the first Marquis of Fronteira, João Mascarenhas, as a hunting lodge. Although strongly influenced by the Italian Renaissance, an influence which is particularly visible in the design of the gardens, this is one of the most beautiful Portuguese buildings, exceptional especially for the quality and diversity of style of its **azulejos★★**.

Within the palace, the *azulejos* of the **Victory Room** evoke major episodes in the War of Restoration, perhaps with some naivety. The dining room is decorated with Delft tiles (17C), the first to be imported into Portugal.

On the terraces and in the **gardens**, glazed tiles have taken over every flat surface, depicting in a rustic style the seasons and work in the fields, and in a grandiose and solemn fashion the 12 horsemen in the Gallery of Kings which are reflected in the waters of the pond. In the humorous scenes, the main characters are cats and monkeys.

One of the busts surrounded by azulejos tiles, in the Palace gardens.

OTHER ATTRACTIONS

Museums

If you are interested in the problems of water supply, the **Museu da Água da EPAL★** (EPAL Water Museum) (DQ M⁵) covers the history of Lisbon's water supply, from the Roman period to the present. The visit will not be complete without having a look at the **Aqueduto das Águas Livres★** (Águas Livres Aqueduct) (ABP), which brings water from 58km (36 miles) away to deliver it to the Mãe d'Água das Amoreiras (CQ K¹), a reservoir which is now out of use.

At the foot of the aqueduct on the pleasant Praça das Amoreiras, the **Fundação Arpad Szenes-Vieira da Silva★** (closed Tuesdays), located in an old silk factory, displays the works of the most Parisian of the

The enormous Roman arches of the Aqueduto das Águas Livres march across the Alcântara Valley.

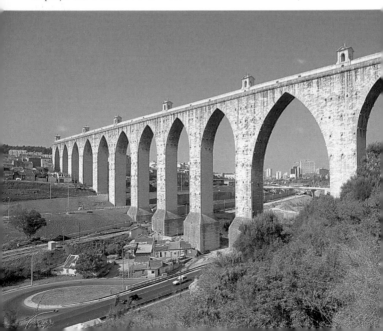

Portuguese painters, and of her husband, the Hungarian Arpad Szenes.

The history of the town is displayed in the **Museu da Cidade** (Municipal Museum) (CN), which is located in the **Pimenta Palace**, an elegant 18C building. The museum traces the history of Lisbon and includes a model of the city before the earthquake. The palace has a kitchen with walls covered in *azulejos*.

The development of Portuguese art between 1850 and 1950 is covered in the **Museu do Chiado★** (KZ), which is located in a 13C convent refurbished by the French architect J-M Wilmotte. All schools are represented: romanticism, naturalism, symbolism and modernism.

Not to be forgotten is the **Museu Militar** (Military Museum) (HY M[15]), where in addition to things military note the splendid woodwork, *azulejos* and **ceilings★**. The **Museu da Música★** (Museum of Music) (BN M[9]), located in the Alto dos Moinhos underground station, has a fine collection of Baroque clavichords. The **Museu Nacional do Traje★** (Museum of Costume) (M[21]) at the Quinta de Monteiro-Mor, to the north of Lisbon, puts on temporary exhibitions. The **Casa Fernando Pessõa** (BQ C[3]) will interest the poet's fans, and the **Museu Rafael Bordalo Pinheiro** (CN M[33]) houses the artist's **ceramics★**.

Churches

The church of **Nossa Senhora de Fátima**, (CP D[2]) not far from the Gulbenkian Museum, is modern but has fine stained-glass **windows★** by Almada Negreiros.

Situated on Graça hill, the church and convent of **Nossa Senhora da Graça** (LX)

A detail of Manueline decoration from the south façade of Igreja da Conceição Velha.

was rebuilt after the earthquake. The rococo interior has fine *azulejos* and you will discover a pretty **view★** from the terrace.

The **south façade★** of the transept of the **Igreja da Conceição Velha** (LZ D) will delight lovers of Manueline art. It was the only part to remain standing after the earthquake.

The 18C **Basílica da Estrela★** (BQ) was built in fine Baroque style, and includes a crib with life-sized characters, the work of Machado de Castro. A notable cupola spans the **transept★**.

Gardens and Parks

Lisbon has many gardens, frequently planted with exotic species brought back from Africa, Asia and Brazil. They offer pleasant walks or shady places to relax. The garden of **Estrela★** (BQ), alongside the basilica, is undoubtedly the most romantic.

The **Jardim Botânico★** (JVX), close to the Academy of Sciences who run it; it has a remarkable subtropical flora and palm tree collection. The **Jardim do Príncipe Real** has an old cypress trimmed into a giant umbrella. The immense **Parque Florestal de Monsanto★** (APQ), which dominates the town, can be visited by car. Set on hills, it provides many lovely views over the city, and numerous routes traverse the huge wooded area. The **Jardim Zoológico★★** (BN) is renowned as both a garden and a zoo. A cable car takes you round the park, passing above the animals, and a small train enables you to see some of the 2 500 species present. The lovely gardens (formal and wild), the views, shows (reptiles, dolphins), temporary exhibitions for children, picnic site and restaurant make it an ideal place to spend a pleasant day. Finally, north of Belém is the romantic **Jardim das Damas** and the **Jardim Botánico da Ajuda★**, with its exotic perfumes.

Part of the dolphin show at the Jardim Zoológico.

EXCURSIONS FROM LISBON

Map of the area surrounding Lisbon.

What about a swim or a visit to the area around Lisbon to round off your visit to the city – distances are short and trains, if not fast, are frequent! (*Cais do Sodré railway station for the coast.*)

Alcobaça★★
110km (68 miles) to the north of Lisbon via the A 8 motorway and the N 8. Museum open daily.
The **Mosteiro de Santa Maria★★** (Monastery of Santa Maria) is a most beautiful Cistercian abbey, dating from 1178. The church, which has been restored to reveal the simplicity of the original Cistercian architecture, contains the **tomb of Inés de Castro★★**, the dead queen. She was assassinated in 1355 on the orders of Afonso IV, who was not happy with her relationship with the crown prince Pedro. Six years later the then King Pedro, whom she had secretly married before her death, had her body exhumed and had her crowned queen. All the members of the

The intricately carved limestone tomb of Inés de Castro.

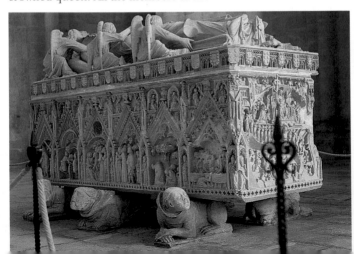

nobility had to kiss the hand of the corpse. **King Pedro's tomb★★** is on the opposite side of the transept.

The **abbey buildings★★** are also worth a visit, in particular the enormous kitchen and the monks' dormitory. In the town, have a look at the blue faïence work in the square, and before heading back to Lisbon sample the local speciality, *ginginha* (cherry brandy).

Mosteiro da Batalha★★★
(Batalha Monastery)

125km (78 miles) to the north of Lisbon, by the A 1 motorway. Open every day.

Set in a green valley, the Monastery of Batalha, was built in the 15C and 16C, before the Jerónimos Monastery in Lisbon, and is a masterpiece of the Gothic and Manueline arts. The **Claustro Real★★★** (Royal Cloisters) are a truly miraculous balance between Gothic simplicity and Manueline stone tracery. The **vaulting★★★** of the **Sala do Capítulo★★** (Chapter House) represents a technical *tour de force* by the architect. Its construction was said to have been so dangerous that only those who had been condemned to death accepted work there as masons. Do not miss the **Capelas Imperfeitas★★** (unfinished chapels), open to the sky, for which the monastery is famous. Begun as a vast mausoleum for King Duarte and his ancestors, it was never completed. A magnificent Gothic porch connects the octagonal room with the church, the **doorway★★** displaying exquisite Manueline decoration.

Cascais★ and Estoril★

25km (15.5 miles) to the west of Lisbon by the A 5 motorway or by the coast road, or by train from

The unfinished chapels of the Batalha Monastery are a masterpiece of Portuguese Gothic and Manueline art.

Cais do Sodré.

Cascais★ combines a traditional fishing harbour with an elegant and cosmopolitan resort, renowned like its neighbour for its favourable climate.

Estoril★ has a famous golf course, is the venue for the Formula One Grand Prix in autumn, and has a modern casino with an enormous hall of one-armed bandits.

Convento de Mafra★★ (Mafra Monastery)

40km (25 miles) to the north-west of Lisbon by the N 117. Closed Tuesdays. One hour guided visit.
The 18C Monastery of Mafra, which is entirely made of marble, was built by a German architect, assisted by Roman artists.

Gold from Brazil financed the building of the **Basilica**★★ and the palace. There is a splendid **library**★, which contains 40 000 works. As for the gigantic Basilica, its sumptuous Baroque decoration and the elegance of its proportions offset its austerity.

Óbidos★★

92km (57 miles) to the north of Lisbon via the A 8 and the N 8, in the direction of Leiria.
In 1282 King Dinis visited the attractive fortified city of Óbidos, and was so delighted with it that he presented it as a gift to his wife, Queen Isabel. The tradition was not broken for six centuries, and it has been given to the current queen of Portugal by her husband. It is a striking white **medieval town**★★, set on a hill overlooking vast green valleys, and enclosed within a **crenelated**

The medieval city of Óbidos still has its perimeter wall of Moorish origins.

wall★★ of Moorish origin. There is a charming *pousada* tucked into the wall which is ideal for a romantic break.

Palácio Nacional de Queluz★★
(Royal Palace of Queluz)

15km (9 miles) to the north-west of Lisbon. 20 minutes by car on the A 5 motorway, turn off towards Oeiras, and then head for Sintra and Queluz. By train from Rossio station on the Sintra line, to Queluz-Belas (20 minutes train, plus a walk of 1km/0.6 miles). Closed on Tuesdays and public holidays.

Built for Queen Maria I, the **Royal Palace** with its rococo façade resembles a small version of the Chateau of Versailles, from which it takes its inspiration. It has retained its 18C furniture and its fine French-style gardens, where the clipped hedges frame masses of flowers, pools and Rococo statues. Do not miss the **Throne Room**★, which is a little like the Hall of Mirrors in Versailles, with its opulent Venetian crystal chandeliers

A sphinx looks out over the French-style gardens of Queluz.

and decorated ceiling. The **Azulejos Room** has polychrome *azulejos* of Chinese and Brazilian landscapes. You can eat in the palace kitchens, which have been converted into a restaurant, and sleep in the outbuildings, which have been converted into a *pousada*.

Sintra★★★

25km (15.5 miles) to the west of Lisbon.
30 mins by car along the A 5 motorway, turn off towards Oeiras, then head for Sintra. By train, from Rossio station (trains leave every 20 mins and take 45 mins). The Royal Palace and Pena Palace are closed on Wednesdays.

Huddled at the foot of the **Serra de Sintra★★**, which the ramparts of the **Castelo dos Mouros** dominate, this small town, dotted with fountains and parks (such as the **Parque da Liberdade**, with its *teatro virtual*) has much to offer the visitor. With its narrow streets lined with aristocratic houses (*quintas*), decorated with *azulejos*, it is obvious why this was the preferred summer residence of the Kings of Portugal.

The **Royal Palace★★**, with its astonishing conical pair of chimneys, is worth a visit. The highlights are its cuisine, the superb **Sala dos Brasoes** (Armoury) with its unusual ceiling and blue and white *azulejos*, and the **Sala das Pegas** (Room of Feet).

The **Museu de Arte Moderna★** (Museum of Modern Art; *closed Mondays and Tuesdays*) has been established in the old casino at Sintra (Av. H. Salgado). It houses the private collection of the financier Berardo. Dubuffet, Stella, Warhol, Robert Indiana, César and many others make up a panorama of artistic creations (1945 to present day).

Perched on the very top of the Serra de Sintra, the **Palácio Nacional da Pena★★**

The Pena Palace is a 19C mixture of architectural styles, built for Ferdinand, husband of Queen Maria II.

Superbly renovated and furnished, Lawrence's – the oldest hotel in the peninsula – has just re-opened after 40 years: ideal for a delightful evening in the steps of Lord Byron!

(Pena Palace), at the edge of the town, is a delightful 19C pastiche, combining almost all styles and enclosing an authentic Manueline cloister. Its terraces provide fine **views**★★ of the region.

Why not extend this charming stop-over by strolling the streets, having a cup of tea in the unusual *Casa de Chá Raposa* (Rua Conde Ferreira 29), or a glass of port or Dão with a *queijada* (sheep's cheese tart) opposite the Palace (*Bar do Binho* and *Loja do Vinho*). Or even spend a night at *Lawrence's* hotel?

Beaches

The most accessible are those along the coast towards **Cascais** and **Estoril** but they are often crowded and sometimes polluted. Be aware, too, that some are dangerous, with strong waves and currents, particularly at **Guincho**, which is very popular with surfers.

When going for a swim, do as the locals do and go a little further, to **Praia das Maçãs** or **Azenhas do Mar** at the foot of the Serra de Sintra, or even **Ericeira**, not far from Mafra. Alternatively, try the beaches on the **Costa da Caparica** to the south of the Tagus, favoured by the Lisbonites (*accessed via the 25 April Bridge, or by boat and bus, and then by a small train that runs along the beaches*). This resort is developing along an enormous stretch of fine sand, where fishermen still carry their nets up the shore on their backs. Join them before stopping off at **Cacilhas**, famous for its fish restaurants.

Estoril, once known as the 'Resort of Kings', is still popular as a beach resort.

One of the best ways of enjoying Lisbon is to use the colourful trams to explore the city.

LISBON LIFE

Living in Lisbon means living like the people of Lisbon. The streets are particularly lively and noisy and are filled with all kinds of pedlars, who will sell you lottery tickets or offer to clean your shoes. You can pass the time in convivial cafés where the cares of the world, great and small, the results of the national football team, the government's policy or local events of the day are discussed in equally serious vein. People still pull their chairs out onto the pavement to enjoy the fresh air while talking with their neighbours, and no one would dream of staying closeted at home to watch television alone – the cafés are there to provide an opportunity for loud comment on the broadcasts. Who cares if no one is watching the programme any more?

Living in Lisbon also means living on foot, at least in the centre of the city. The traffic is quite anarchic and chaotic, and finding somewhere to park is guaranteed to be a challenge. The city is not all that big, and with the underground, buses, funiculars, trams and the *cacilheiros* (the boats which cross the Tagus) it is well served with public transport.

DISCOVERING THE CITY

Although Lisbon is small enough to explore much of the city centre on foot, there are a number of guided tour options which take the slog out of it, especially when the temperatures soar in the summer months.

A good way to discover Lisbon is to catch, from the Praça do Comércio, the **eléctrico de turismo**, the venerable hundred-year-old tram which, from 20 March to 18 October, tours the Alfama and Bairro Alto districts.
Departure times:
March-June: 1.30pm, 3.30pm
Oct: 11.30am, 1.30pm, 2.30pm, 3.30pm
July-Aug: as March-June with an extra tour planned at 4.30pm
Sept: 11.30am, 1.30pm, 3.30pm
Guaranteed to be fun!

A more conventional way to explore the city is by **coach – Cityrama**. Departing from the Praça Marques de Pombal, there are various options: half-day tours of the city, daily at 9am and 2pm (5 250$); night tours, including a *fado* restaurant, on Monday, Wednesday and Friday at 8pm; excursions to the coast (Estoril) or Sintra, etc. For further information and reservations ☎ 21 319 10 91 or ☎ 21 386 43 22.

Prices are similar to coach excursions by **Gray Line**. These depart daily from Pombal, at 9am and 2.30pm. The company also organises night tours and excursions beyond Lisbon ☎ 21 357 00 60.

Cruises on the Tagus
Organised by the company **Transtejo** (☎ 21 882 03 48), cruises on the Tagus (Cruzeiros no Tejo) leave from the quay, Terreiro do Paço, opposite the Praça do Comércio.

From April to October, cruises depart at 11am and 3pm, and last two hours. From November to March they depart at 3pm and last 1hour 45 minutes. Tickets (adults: 3 000$; children 6-12 years: 1 500$) can be purchased from the kiosk on the Praça do Comércio, on the Tagus.

And Beyond the City...
Travel agencies offer coach tours to areas and attractions outside Lisbon itself, but it is far preferable to make these

excursions by yourself. Even if you do not have a vehicle, Estoril and Cascais are accessible by train (a 30-minute journey from Cais do Sodré, with trains leaving every 20 minutes until 2.30am). For Sintra and the north of Lisbon, leave from the Estaçao do Rossio. Mafra, however, is served by coaches only.

WEATHER

Lisbon benefits from a mild climate almost the whole year round, only dropping to 10-13°C (50-56°F) in winter. It is particularly pleasant in May and June, and in September and October, with temperatures around 20°C (68°F). However, in July and August temperatures reach 30°C (86°F); the heat and the invasion of tourists can make sightseeing an exhausting experience, so avoid this period when visiting the city if you can. The nights remain cool because of the sea breeze from the Atlantic.

A sunny city, the Queen of the Tagus receives an average of 686mm (27in) of rain every year, and is particularly wet between December and March. In winter, there are frequent fogs, wind and humidity, but snow is unknown in Lisbon.

CALENDAR OF EVENTS

Popular Saints' Days: 13 June is a holiday in Lisbon in honour of the patron saint of the city, St Anthony. The festival begins the evening before: folklore groups (*marchas populares*) descend the Avenida da Liberdade to the accompaniment of music, while in the squares decorated with fairy lights – particularly in the districts of Alfama, Mouraria and Bairro Alto – there is dancing, with grilled sardines (*sardinhas*) and snails (*caracol*) to be eaten, and lovers offer each other basil. Whatever you do, do not smell it by putting your nose over it, this brings bad luck! Rub the leaves and breathe the perfume from your hand – it's a holy plant.

The 'popular saints' – St John, St Peter and St Vincent – are fêted every evening by local dances lasting up to the end of the month of June.

Apart from public holidays (*see* p.123), there are other key events and festivals:
6 March: procession of the Senhor dos Passos à Graça.
Good Friday: procession of the Way of the Cross, particularly in the Bairro Alto.
27-29 June: feast of St Peter at Sintra.
July and August: craft fair from all the regions of Portugal, in

Some of the more traditional houses and hotels are richly decorated with azulejos.

Estoril.

24 July to 8 August: St James's fair in Setubal, with *touradas* and folklore groups.

2nd Sunday in August: *touradas*, folk dancing and fireworks for the Fishermen's Festival in Alcochete.

ACCOMMODATION

Lisbon offers a wide choice of accommodation, ranging from **youth hostels** (*pousada de juventude*) for those on a tight budget to luxury hotels (*estalagem*). Between these extremes you can choose from modest **boarding-houses** (*pensão*), or *residencials*, which are slightly more comfortable but have no restaurant and are not necessarily any cleaner.

In general, for the same standard, prices are very much lower here than in other European capitals. **Hotels** are officially classified from one-star to five-star. Whether the hotel has a restaurant or not, the price of breakfast (*pequenho almoço*) is generally included in the price of the room (*quarto*).

During the season or when international events are on, prices are higher and it is advisable to book in advance. To give you an idea of prices, a double room in a luxury hotel will cost around 40 000$. Comfortable hotels charge around 20 000-30 000$ a night, while more modest hotels ask between 10 000-15 000$. At a camping site or in a youth hostel you can expect to pay around 5 000$.

If you wish to stay in a **youth hostel**, contact the Youth Hostel Association (YHA) in Great Britain ☎ 0870 870 8808, Fax 01727 844 126; or in Lisbon the *Pousada de Juventude*, Rua Andrade Corvo 46, Saldanha (Underground Picoas) (☎/Fax 213 53 26 96 and 2134 13 88 20). If you are making an excursion, there is also a youth hostel in Sintra, Santa Eufémia, (☎/Fax 219 24 12 40). Do not forget to obtain an international pass before leaving home.

Many tour operators offer interesting and competitive package deals, which combine an air ticket with hotel bookings. You can obtain details from your travel agent.

For information on hotels and restaurants, consult the *Michelin Red Guide Portugal* and the *Michelin Red Guide to Spain and Portugal*. These guides, which are updated every year, offer a selection of hotels, from the simplest to the most luxurious, classified by district and according to comfort.

Several Good Addresses

Around 50 000$

Four Seasons H. The Lisbon Ritz *Rua Rodrigo da Fonseca 88, 1099-039 Lisbon* (☎ 21 383 20 20, Fax 21 383 17 83). A luxurious hotel, which is justly famous. Not far from the Eduardo VII Park, with magnificent views over the city.

From 25 000$ to 40 000$

York House *Rua das Janelas Verdes 32, 1200 Lisbon* (☎ 21 396 25 44, Fax 21 397 27 93). Located in a superb ancient buildings – a 16C convent – close to the Museum of Ancient Art. Fine food: meals can be taken in the shade of a magnificent palm tree.

As Janelas Verdes *Rua das Janelas Verdes 47, 1200 Lisbon* (☎ 21 396 81 43, Fax 21 396 81 44) Set in a late 17C mansion, close to the Museum of Ancient Art. No restaurant.

Hotel Real Parque Av. Luis Bivar 67, 1069 Lisbon(☎ 21 357 01 01, Fax 21 357 07 50).

Not far from the Calouste Gulbenkian Foundation and the Eduardo VII Park; a comfortable, modern establishment with an annexe, the **Real Residencia** (Rua Ramalho Ortigão 41 ☎ 21 382 29 00).

From 15 000$ to 25 000$
Metrópole Hotel *Praça do Rossio 30, 1100 Lisbon* (☎ 21 346 91 64, Fax 21 346 91 66).
Could not be more central!
Albergaria Senhora do Monte *Calçada do Monte 39, 1170-250 Lisbon* (☎ 21 886 60 02, Fax 21 887 77 83).
Superb view of St George's Castle and the Tagus.
Veneza *Avenida da Liberdade 189, 1250 Lisbon* (☎ 21 352 26 18, Fax 21 352 66 78).
A charming establishment, Ventian-style, of course!
Da Torre *Rua dos Jerónimos 8, 1400-211 Lisbon* (☎ 21 363 62 62, Fax 21 364 59 95).
Opposite the monastery in Belém; ideal if you are travelling by car.

Around 10 000$
Hotel Borges *Rua Garrett 108, 1200-205 Lisbon* (☎ 21 346 19 51, Fax 21 342 66 17).
Superbly situated in the heart of Chiado... but it could do with some renovating!
Residéncia Roma *Travessa da Glória 22-A, 1250 Lisbon* (☎/Fax 21 346 05 57).
Simple establishment, near the Praça dos Restauradores.
Horizonte *Av António Augusto de Aguiar 42* (☎ 21 353 95 26, Fax 21 353 84 74)·
Simple and well-run; located opposite the superb underground station, Parque.
Pensão São João de Praça *Rua São João da Praça, 1100-519 Lisbon* (☎ 21 886 25 91, Fax 21 888 13 78).
One of the few places to stay in the Alfama district, near the Sé. Quiet... and some rooms on the third floor have a superb view over the Tagus.

Further Afield

Óbidos: For a fun adventure in Óbidos, the **Pousada do Castelo** (*Paço Real* ☎ 26 295 91 05, Fax 26 295 91 48), located in the castle ramparts, is unrivalled! Or you might prefer to stay in an old convent, the **Estalagem do Convento** (*Rua D. João d'Ornelas* ☎ 26 295 92 16, Fax 26 295 91 59), or perhaps an old residence such as the **Casa do Relógio** (*Rua da Graça* ☎/Fax 26 295 92 82), which is far cheaper.

Sintra: You can enjoy the natural surroundings of the Sintra forest if you stay in the marvellous **Quinta da Capela**

(4.5km from Sintra, on the road to Colares ☎ 21 929 01 70, Fax 21 929 34 25) or, if you really want to go to town, why not choose the castle. **Palácio de Seteais** (*Rua Barbosa do Bocage 8* ☎ 21 923 32 00, Fax 21 923 42 77). You will definitely succumb to the charm of **Lawrence's**, a stone's throw away from the Palais Royal (*Rua Consigliéri Pedroso 38* ☎ 21 910 55 00, Fax 21 910 55 05).

Cascais: If you prefer the sea, the beautiful **Casa da Pérgola** (*Avenida Valbom 13* ☎ 21 484 00 40, Fax 21 483 47 91) is an old stately home.

FOOD AND DRINK

Soup is rarely missing from a meal. The best known is *caldo verde*, based on kale and potatoes, with a floating slice of sausage, but other traditional soups include chicken and rice (*canja de galinha*), fish (*sopa de peixe*), sea food (*sopa de marisco*), rabbit (*sopa de coelho*), or chick peas (*sopa de grão*). Bread soups (*açordas*) contain coriander leaves, olive oil, garlic, bread and a poached egg, and almost always feature on the menu. *Gaspacho*, a sharp soup containing tomatoes, onions, cucumbers and peppers, is served chilled with toasted

A classic Portuguese display of seafood and cheeses.

croutons.

A maritime country, Portugal is rich in **fish**. Cod (*bacalhau*) is the most common, and there are, it is said, 365 ways of preparing it. You can also feast on grilled sardines, garlic clams, swordfish, lampreys, shad from the Tagus, fillets of Algarve tuna, or 'caldeirada', a kind of bouillabaisse.

Seafood (*mariscos*) and octopus (*polvo*) are abundant, and garnish many dishes. Shellfish, always cooked, are delicious and varied. Prawns (*lagosta*) cooked in the manner of Peniche (on the coast near Lisbon) – braised on the fire – are famous.

As for **meat**, pork is prepared in a variety of ways: stewed, in smoked tongue sausages (*linguiça*), in smoked fillets, and as smoked ham (*presunto*). Accompanied by red or white beans, cabbage and sausage, ham is one of the ingredients of the *feijoada*. Ham and sausages are included in the preparation of the *cozido à portuguesa*, a stew of beef, vegetables, potatoes and rice. Beef is frequently eaten in the form of steak.

There are many tasty sheep's **cheeses** to sample (from October to May). Try the Serra da Estrela (*queijo da Serra*), Castelo Branco, or Azeitão, which is very creamy. There are goats' cheeses such as the *queijos secos* (dry cheeses), and the *cabreiro*. The small white cheeses (*quejinhos*) from Tomar are often served as an hors-d'œuvre, as is the fresh goats' cheese, *queijo fresco*.

You will discover all kinds of **pastries**, almost all based on eggs, and many inherited from old convent recipes such as the *Toucinho-do-Céu* (heavenly lard cake) and *Barriga-de-Freira* (Nun's belly). The *pudim flan* is a sort of custard. The *leite-creme* is like the flan, but more creamy. *Arroz doce* (rice pudding) is served dusted with cinnamon at festive meals.

In the cake shops, of which there are many in Lisbon, a particular delicacy is *pastéis de nata* – a custard in flaky pastry, dusted with cinnamon.

Wines

Portugal has a very rich range of wines of excellent quality, at very affordable prices. In restaurants you will certainly find **vinho verde** on offer – a white wine whose name 'green wine' is indicative of its youth and a short fermentation that yields a wine of low alcohol content. Light, slightly sparkling, fruity, and even slightly sharp, it is served chilled. You will also find the fresh white wine and the very soft, velvety and flavoursome red wine, similar to Burgundy, which comes from the valley of the Dão; Colares, the robust red from the Serra de Sintra; Bucelas, a sharp, dry, straw-yellow white wine produced on the banks of the River Trancão, a tributary of the Tagus; the red wines of the Ribatejo, Cartaxo; the whites of Chamusca, Almeirim and Alpiarça; and the rosés of Pinhel and Mateus. **Vinho da casa**, house wine, is also usually very acceptable.

To accompany dessert, the moscatel from Setúbal is a generous fruity wine, which acquires a particularly pleasant flavour with age.

Port

The best known of Portuguese wines, port is produced in northern Portugal from the Douro region, on schisty soil which gives it its unique characteristics. The wine ferments at the vineyard until Douro brandy is added before it is transported to the cellars at

Choosing from the wide range of ports on sale can be fun.

Vila Nova da Gaia, in the suburbs of Oporto. There, it ages in enormous vats and then in wooden barrels. The alcohol content is approximately 20%. There are different types of ports.

Porto Branco (white port), the least known, is produced from white grapes. A dry wine, it is an excellent aperitif when served chilled.

Blended ports are red ports obtained from blends of vineyards and years whose secrets the producers guard jealously. Blending and ageing depend on the quality of the port which is required. This can yield the **tinto** or **red** which, young and full bodied, is very fruity, and the commonest. Blends from different vineyards and different years yield **ruby** or **tinto alourado**, which retains fine vigour despite the ageing. Pale and softened with age, it takes on a golden yellow colour and is named **alourado** or **tawny**. Finally, it becomes a clear yellow and is the **alourado claro** or **light tawny**, the finest of the fine.

Street life in central Lisbon is lively, with its pedestrian streets and open-air cafés.

Restaurants and Cafés

The districts most frequented for their restaurants are the Bairro Alto, the Baixa, Alfama, Madragoa and Belém. Cafés are the places to go for a *bica* (black coffee), accom-panied by *pastéis de nata* (pastries). The best known are in the Rossio (Nicola), Praça Figueira (Confeitaria Nacional), Rua Garrett (Pastelaria Benard), Rua Dom Pedro V (Mássima), and Belém (Antigua Confeitaria de Belém).

A Small Selection...

The *Michelin Red Guide Portugal* offers a wide choice of restaurants in Lisbon, classified by district and rating. Here are a few you may like to try:

Over 6 000$

Tágide (Largo da Académia Nacional de Belas Artes 18 ☎ 21 342 07 20; *closed Saturday and Sunday*)
The upstairs room is decorated with *azulejos* and has a magnificent view over the Tagus. Good traditional cooking.

Tavares (Rua da Misericórdia 37 ☎ 21 342 11 12; *closed Saturday lunchtime and Sunday*)
A turn-of-the-century atmosphere.

Vela Latina (Doca do Bom Sucesso ☎ 21 301 71 18; *closed Sunday*)
A superb location on a marina, near the Tower of Belém.

Casa da Comida (Travessa das Amoreiras 1, Rato underground, then take the *calçada* Bento da Rocha Cabral ☎ 21 388 53 76; *closed Saturday lunchtime and Sunday*)
The fish is excellent and the patio is full of flowers!

Mãe d'Água (Travessa das Amoreiras 10 ☎ 21 388 28 20; *closed Sunday*)
Close to the Vieira da Silva Foundation; decorated with engravings of bullfights.

From 4 000$ to 6 000$
Caseiro (Rua de Belém 35 ☎ 21 363 88 03; *closed Sunday and in August*)
Portuguese cooking in a rustic setting, close to the Jerónimos Monastery.

Delfim (Rua Nova de São Mamede 25 ☎ 21 383 05 32; *closed Saturday*)
A local establishment, where the portions are very generous; near the Botanical Gardens.

Ja Sei (Avenida Brasilia 1400 ☎ 21 301 59 69)
On a small lake between the Jerónimos Monastery and the Monument to the Discoveries.

Casa do Alentejo (Rua das Portas de Sto Antão 58, Restauradores underground; *closed from 19 July to 2 August*)
Specialities from the Alentejo are served in this incredible palace in the Baiza district (cross the Moorish patio to get to the rooms upstairs).

Verdemar (Rua das Portas de Sto Antão 142 ☎ 21 346 44 01)
A fish restaurant, which has the advantage of being open on Sunday.

Less than 4 000$
D'Avis (Rua do Grilo 98 ☎ 21 868 13 54; *closed Sunday and first two weeks of August*)
Good value; traditional cooking from the Alentejo, served in a typical décor. Near the Madre de Deus.

Lautasco (Beco Azinhal 7-7A ☎ 21 886 01 73; *closed Sunday*)
Near the Casa do Fado e da Guitarra Portuguese, at the foot of Alfama, a *tasca* where you can eat well.

Cervejaria Portugália (Av. Almirante Reis 117 ☎ 21 314 00 02; *closed public holidays*)
One of the best brasseries in Lisbon.

Martinho da Arcada (Plaça do Comércio 3 ☎ 21 886 62 13; *closed Sunday*)
For Pessõa fans!

Antigo Farta Brutos (Travessa da Espera 20 ☎ 21 342 67 56; *closed Saturday lunchtime and Sunday*)

Traditional cooking in the Bairro Alto; considered to be one of the most reputable places to go.

A Primavera (Travessa da Espera 34 ☎ 21 342 04 77; *closed Sunday*)
You have to elbow your way into this tiny restaurant!

Not to be forgotten are the **museum cafeterias**, often in pleasant settings. This is particularly true of the Belém Cultural Centre, the Museum of Decorative Arts and especially the Museum of Azulejos, with its patio full of plants!

Where to have a drink?

In the **Alfama**, **Cerca Mouras** (Largo Porta do Sol) has magnificent views over the Tagus. **Chapitó** (Rua Costa do Castelo 1/7; *closed Sunday*) set in a circus school on one of the most pleasant terraces in the city, serves *tapas* at all times of the day. **O Salvador** (Rua Salvador 53) is known for its cocktails, whilst the **Bar da Graça** (Travessa Pereira 43) welcomes music, theatre and art enthusiasts.

In the **Baixa**, **Ginginha do Rossio** (Largo S. Domingo 8) offers the opportunity to discover cherry brandy (*ginginha*) in a unique atmosphere. Those who love the drink can also enjoy it in the Rua das Portas de São Antão at no 7 (**Ginginha Sem Rival**) and at no 61 (**Ginhinha Popular**), which are just as picturesque. Full of history, **Café Nicola** (Rua 1° Dezembro 20) is one of the most trendy spots in Lisbon.

In the **Bairro Alto** and **Chiado**, you are spoilt for choice! A few favourites around the Praça Luís de Camões include: **A Brasileira** (Rua Garrett 120), an institution, and its neighbour the **Pastelaria Benard** (at no 104), also a traditional haunt; **Artis** (Rua Diário Noticias 95-97), famous for its jazz, moscatel and a collection of wind instruments; the **Café No Chiado** (Rua Ivens), located in a patio of the

A crowded antique shop in Rua Dom Pedro V, Bairro Alto.

restored Chiado (access through the porch at no 57). At Rua São Pedro de Alcântara, opposite the miradouro of the same name, the **Solar do Vinho Porto** offers a variety of local wines, to be sampled in an elegant, subdued atmosphere. Further along, a former grocer's shop, the **Pavilhão Chinés** (Rua Dom Pedro V 89) has astonishing collections of all kinds.

The **Cais do Sodré** is the meeting place for lovers of beer, with Guinness *de rigueur* in the **O'Gillins Irish Pub** (Rua dos Remolares 8) and the **Hennessy Irish Pub** (Rua do Cais do Sodré 32/38). You can sample 'Ginger Beer', which has been drawn from the keg since 1918 at the **British Bar** (Rua Bernardino Costa 52; *closed Sunday*).

SHOPPING

The most commercial districts are the Baixa (Rua Augusta) and the Chiado (Rua Garrett), where there are large numbers of traditional clothing, craftwork and jewellery shops. The Bairro Alto is where the trendsetters have established themselves, and also has some some very fine bookshops.

Those looking for **shopping centres** might like to try Armazéms do Chiado (access Rua do Carmo), the Amoreiras Towers, or the Espaço Chiado (where you can see remains of 14C fortifications). However, the biggest is the Centro Vasco da Gama (Oriente underground).

Recommendations

Antique shops are grouped together along the Rua São Bento – between the Parliament and the Rato – and the Ruas Dom Pedro V and Escola Politécnica. Here you will find ceramics, *azulejos* and furniture, or go to the *Feira da Ladra* on Tuesdays and Saturdays. If you are in the

Pottery, such as this attractive faïence (made from white clay), can be a good buy.

Houses decorated with azulejos in the narrow stepped lanes of the Alfama district.

Baixa, drop by the Abside shop (Travessa dos Fiés de Deus 14-16). You can also find very fine antiques in Sintra.

If you are interested in Portuguese haute couture and its talented designers, check out the **fashion** in these boutiques: José António Tenente (Travessa do Carmo 8) and Bazar Paraíso (Rua do Norte 42), both in the Bairro Alto; José Carlos (Travessa do Monte Carmo 2, Príncipe Real); Ana Salazar (Rua do Carmo 87/Ave de Roma 16E).

Craftwork offers a remarkable variety of products, from the rustic to the extremely refined. For regional products, crafts and souvenirs, call in at Manteigaria Londrina (Rua Portas Sto Antonio 53); Manuel Tavares (Lda, Rua da Betesga

Azulejos outside a shop depicting ladies making traditional embroidered cloths.

1A-1B); or Artesanato (Rua Castilho 61B, Liberdade).

Pottery is a good buy, glazed in bright colours and decorated with branches and flowers or geometrical patterns. Pieces sometimes take on unexpected shapes: water pots, salad bowls, plates laden with a decoration of leaves, flowers, animals. Very pretty multicoloured cocks are also made. Portuguese

porcelain has a long tradition of producing some very fine pieces, and the tradition is still going strong today. Go and see it displayed at Vista Alegre (Largo do Chiado 18).

The **crystal glassware** from Marinha Grande is sold in Rua São Bento (Nos 234-242), while Atlantis Crystal is sold at Rua Ivens (No 48).

Azulejos are still

manufactured by traditional methods. You will find a good range in the shop of the National Azulejos Museum, and in those of the Workshops of Sant'Anna (Rua do Alecrim 91-95, Chiado), Viúvia Lamego (Largo do Intendente 25) and Santa Rufina (Rua Conde de Panafiel 9). You can also try Albuquerque e Sousa Lda (Rua D Pedro V 70, Bairro Alto); Constância (Rua S Domingos 8, Lapa); or for designs by contemporary artists, try Ratton (Rua Academia das Ciências 2C, Príncipe Real) or in the A Oficina Arcade (Largo de S Rafael 1), in the Alfama. Some antique shops in Rua Dom Pedro V also have *azulejos*.

Madeira **table cloths** are renowned, but marvellously embroidered linen shawls and bedspreads also make lovely souvenirs. Handmade embroidery and lace can be bought at the famous Príncipe Real (12-14 Rua de Escola Politécnica), at Teresa Alecrim

(Rua Nova do Almada 76), and at Madeira House (Rua Augusta 133, Baixa).

Thanks to its great malleability, gold filigree is used to make **jewellery** in the form of hearts, crosses, earrings and brooches.

The **carpets** and **tapestries** of Portalegre are a pride of the country. Trevo (Av Óscar Monteiro Torres 33A, Praça de Touros) specialises in Arraiolos carpets.

There are a multitude of

The colourful stalls at Feira da Ladra, Alfama.

painted wooden objects in the traditional craftwork of Portugal. Toys, in particular, are a good buy, and are found in the shops of Belém and Sintra.

Fado records make an evocative souvenir to remind you of your visit. There are so many to choose from, but do not be shy about asking for advice. The best selection is at the Discoteca do Carmo (Rua do Carmo 63). There are countless recordings of **Amália Rodrigues**, the great interpreter of *fado*, who died in October 1999. Apart from the wonderful and complete *Segredo* (EMI), released in 1997, you will find a number of her compilations.

Leather is of good quality in Portugal. For shoes and bags, go to the Rua Augusta, Rua Garrett and, not far from Eduardo VII Park, Rua Castilho, and you will find thousands of gloves in a tiny specialist shop, Luvaria Ulisses (Rua do Carmo).

You can purchase a few bottles of **port** at the Mercearia Nacional (Rua dos Douradores), or at Casa Macário (Rua Augusta), or at the **Instituto do Vinho do Porto** (which has a shop at the airport – handy for last-minute purchases!).

Finally, for those who prefer American-style shopping

centres, there is a luxurious modern commercial centre in the **Amoreiras Towers** (Av Eng Duarte Pacheco).

Markets

If you are looking for local colour, take a turn round one of the many markets in Lisbon and its surroundings – an ideal way to get a feel for the town, and maybe pick up a bargain on the way!

Feira da Ladra, Campo Sta Clara, Alfama (*Tues, 7am-1pm; Sat 7am-6pm*)

Mercado da Ribeira Nova, Av 24 de Julho (*Mon-Sat, 6am-2pm*)

Feira de Sintra, Largo de São Pedro, at Sintra (*second and fourth Sunday of the month, all year*)

Feira de Cascais, near the shore at Cascais (*first and third Sunday of the month, all year*)

ENTERTAINMENT AND NIGHTLIFE

Lisbon's nightlife often goes on till very late. It is normal to begin the evening with a stop in a café, after dinner, for a *bica* (small coffee), before going on to further adventures. There will be little chance for such in the **Baixa**: once the shops and offices have closed, the neighbourhood recovers an astonishing calm after the bustle of the working day. Instead, you should go to the **Bairro Alto,** which has become the 'hip' district of Lisbon since it was invaded by the artistic and intellectual circles of the capital.

There is something there for all tastes, from *fado* houses to cybercafés, from gay discotheques (the latter are particularly common in the residential district of the **Príncipe Real**) and jazz clubs, to countless often colourful bars. Worth a visit is **Frágil** (Rua Atalaia 126-8), an institution of Lisbon nightlife, **Targus** (Rua Diário de Notícias 40B) or, for the younger set, the metallic **Captain Kirk** (Rua do Norte 121). Those who hold to tradition will go to **Alfama** where, although *fado* is always king, Brazilian music has a high profile.

Along the Tagus, towards Bélem, the districts of the Avenida 24 de Julho and the Docks will also satisfy the lovers of techno music and rock, salsa and Afro-Cuban rhythms (though you have to go there by car). One of the most famous nightclubs has set up in the old Alcântara maritime terminal. The more adventurous might haunt the sailors' taverns and bars of the Cais do Sodré, and, who knows, perhaps you might experience the famous *saudade* ...

To find out what's on, buy the magazine *SE7e*, which is in Portuguese and comes out on Wednesdays, or obtain the *Agenda Cultural*, a monthly publication (in English and Portuguese), which is distributed free in hotels and at the Tourist Office.

Cinema

There are several cinemas on the Avenida da Liberdade and in the commercial centre of Amoreiras. As on television, films are shown in the original version, subtitled in Portuguese. Cinema-goers will enjoy an evening at the **Cinemateca Portuguesa** (Rua Barata Salgueiro 39, Av da Liberdade) which also offers old films and avant-garde Portuguese films.

Discos

Most of the discos in Lisbon are to be found on the Avenida 24 de Julho (**Kapital**, **Xafarix**, **A Paulinha**, etc.) and, not far away, in the district of Alcântara (**Alcântara Mar**, **Salsa Latina**), Doca Sto Amaro Amaro (**5 ao Rio**, **7 Mares**, **Cais S**, **Doca de Santo**), and Amazém (**Ultramar**, **Speakeasy**, **Rock City**, etc.), to name but a few.

The oldest **jazz** joint in Lisbon is the **Hot Clube**, located in Praça Alegria.

Those who like African rhythms – particularly those of Cape Verde – should go to **A Lontra** (Rua do São Bento 155) or the **Ritz Clube** (Rua da Glória 57).

The hotspots for Brazilian music in the city are in the Alfama/Graça district: the **Bruxa Bar** (Rua São Mamede Caldas 35), the **Pé Sujo** (Lg. São Marinho 6-7), and the **Bar Anos 60** (Lg. Terreirinho 21).

Fado

If you wish to hear *fado*, the most characteristic entertainment which Lisbon has to offer, ask the locals where to go for the best *fado*. Among the most well-known clubs, you could try **Adega do Ribatejo** (Rua Diário Notícias 23, in the Bairro Alto), **Senhor Vinho** (Rua Meio a Lapa 18), **Cabacinha** (Largo Limoeiro 9-10, in Alfama) or the **Taverna del Rei** (Largo de Chafariz de Dentro 15).

Theatre and Music

There are a number of theatres in Lisbon, notably the **Teatro Nacional São Carlos** (Rua Serpa Pinto), the **São Luis Theatre** (Rua Antonio Maria Cardoso), the **Dona Maria II National Theatre** (Praça Dom Pedro IV), the **Gulbenkian Centre** (CP) which offers concerts, ballets and plays, and the **Belém Cultural Centre** (Praça do Império) which also offers classical music, concerts and ballets. The **Coliseu dos Recreios** (Rua Portas St Anão, Baixa), with its 5 000-seat auditorium, offers a varied programme of entertainment.

You can obtain tickets for performances at the 'ABEP' kiosk, in Praça dos Restauradores, or at the 'Quiosque Cultural' in S. Mamede, Rue São Mamede, Príncipe Real.

Equestrian Events

Portugal maintains a well-established tradition of riding, not only on account of the bullfights, in which the horse, of the Lusitanian breed, is one of the key performers, but also because of the **Portuguese School of Equestrian Art**. Established in 1979, this prestigious academy is the successor not only to the Royal Riding School founded in the late 16C, but also the *Picaria Reale*, which uses Lusitanian horses from the old royal stud founded in 1748 by King João V.

Today, against the background of the Queluz National Palace, horsemen dressed in 18C costumes give gala performances (*every Wednesday from April to October, except in August* ☎ 21 435 89 15) where the traditions of Portuguese Haute École can be appreciated.

SPORTS

Football matches are very popular in Portugal and on match days Lisbon looks like a ghost town. The city's two teams, Benfica and Sporting, are widely supported, and tickets can be difficult to come by as there are so many season-ticket holders. The two football grounds, Benfica and Lumiar, are located to the north of the city and games are played on Sunday afternoons.

Another spectator sport which is almost as fanatically followed is **bullfighting**. Every Thursday evening, from May to September, a *tourada* takes place at the **Praça de Touros do Campo Pequeno** (Avenida da Republica, Campo Pequeno). Details can be obtained from the Tourist Information Office.

Tourada is the Portuguese version of the bullfight which, unlike its Spanish counterpart, has retained its original characteristics. Most importantly, it takes place on horseback, and the bulls, whose horns are 'blunted' (covered with a leather sheath), are not killed in the arena but are slaughtered in the bull pen after the fight.

A *tourada* generally consists of a fight between six bulls and three horsemen, the *cavaleiros*, dressed in a gold embroidered jacket and wearing a three-cornered hat. The *cavaleiros* are accompanied by *peãos* (helpers) who position the bull with their capes, or keep it away from the horse if there is any danger. The object is to place darts (*farpas*) and banderillas (*ferros*) in the bull's back, while avoiding contact with the bull and complying with a number of rules.

In Lisbon, *touradas* take place in the Praça de Touros, on the Campo Pequeno, a neo-Moorish building which seats 8 000.

Each different way of approaching the bull (the *sortes*) has a name, and the most admired horseman is the one who positions the bull for his *sortes* himself, fights without wasting time or making 'empty passes' (without being able to place his darts), and can vary his angles of attack. The quick circling by the horses and the mastery of the horseman make this part of the event quite spectacular.

After doing his bit, the horseman hands over to the *forcados* who have to gain mastery over the bull, and grace and elegance give way to cruder tactics. These eight men stand behind each other in a line, facing the bull, and attract its attention by shouting and jumping. When the bull charges the leading man, he throws himself between its horns and attempts to overcome it, while the next two seize the horns and a third grabs the animal's tail. This is the *pega*, which is often quite violent (not infrequently the *forcados* get a good shaking) and is considered to be a success if the animal is immobilised

The Penha Longa Golf Club has an 18-hole course designed by Robert Trent Jones.

rapidly. Once released, it is returned to the bull pen with the help of a group of oxen.

In Lisbon, *touradas* take place between Easter and October in the arena (Praça de Touros) on the **Campo Pequeno**, a neo-Moorish building which seats 8 000.

For those who prefer to take a more active role, there are ample opportunities for **watersports**. **Sailing** is widespread along the Atlantic coast and in the Tagus estuary, and the waters around Lisbon are popular locations for **windsurfing**, with board hire available locally. The Costa de Lisboa, from Setúbal to Cabo da Roca, offers a variety of beaches for **swimming** and lazing in the sun (*see* p.86).

There is a wide selection of **golf** courses to choose from, several of a very high standard. Details can be obtained from the Tourist Information Office.

THE BASICS

Before You Go

Strictly speaking, travellers from EU countries do not need a passport to enter Portugal, but it is advisable to bring it along, particularly for drivers, who will receive an on-the-spot fine if they fail to produce it at the request of the authorities. A passport is also the only form of identification accepted at some casinos. Visitors from certain Commonwealth countries will need a visa, as will holders of British, Irish and US passports planning to stay in Portugal longer than three months.

Vaccinations are not required for visitors from Europe or North America. Travellers from areas where cholera or smallpox is present may be required to produce vaccination certificates.

Getting There

By Air BA and TAP Air Portugal (the national airline) operate daily scheduled flights from London (Heathrow) to Lisbon (2½hrs), and TAP also flies from Manchester. In season, there may be last-minute bargain charter flights available; contact the airlines or your travel agent for details of these and fly-drive offers:

BA ☎ (0345) 222111
TAP, Gillingham House, 38-44 Gillingham St, London SW1V 1HU ☎ 0171 828 0260
From US: (toll-free) ☎ 800 221 7370
For information in Lisbon ☎ 21 840 2060.
TAP also operates non-stop flights from Newark and New York to Lisbon, and TWA from New York to Lisbon, but it can be cheaper for visitors from the US to fly to London or Madrid first, and then on to Lisbon. For information and reservations, contact:
TAP Air Portugal, Rua Duque de Palmela 23-3°
☎ 21 317 91 00 or at the airport ☎ 21 841 50 00.
The Portela International Airport at Sacavém is 6km (3.7 miles) north of the town centre. The Aerobus leaves the airport every 20 minutes (7am-9pm). It crosses the city centre to Cais do Sodré railway station. Main stops: Campo Pequeno, Marques de Pombal, Av Liberdade, Restauradores, Rossio and Praça Comércio. Allow 20-45 mins travelling time, depending on traffic. Tickets are valid for one or three days, on all public transport in the city. If you travel by TAP, show your air ticket: the bus trip to the airport is then free.

By Train A daily train service operates between London (Victoria) and Lisbon, via Paris and Irun in northern Spain, but the journey can take over 40 hours. Taking the Eurostar to Paris reduces the journey time considerably. Schedule information and reservations are available from British Railways, (International Section), Victoria Station, London SW1V 1JY ☎ **0171 834 2345**. French Railways (SNCF) operate many high-speed passenger trains and motorail services throughout France. Contact French Railways, 179 Piccadilly, London W1V 0BA ☎ **0171 409 3518**.

By Car Cross-channel car and passenger services from the UK are numerous for those wanting to drive to Portugal (approximately 2 100km/ 1 300 miles from the French ports to Lisbon) and there is a car ferry service between Plymouth and Santander – the journey takes 24 hours – in northern Spain (about 965km/600 miles drive to Lisbon). There are no direct ferry services between Britain and Portugal.

By Coach Eurolines run from Victorial Coach Station. For information ☎ **(0990) 14 32 19** or **(01582) 40 45 11**.

A-Z

Accidents and Breakdowns

If you are in a hire car, the rental company should be able to assist you so carry their details with you at all times. In the event of breakdown in your own car, the Portuguese Automobile Club (Autómovel Clube de Portugal) can be called upon. Their head office is in Rua Rosa Araújo 24, Lisboa 1200 ☎ **21 356 39 31**. Accidents should be reported to the police.

Accommodation see p.90

Airports see Getting There, p.112

Banks

Banks are usually open from 8.30am-2.45/3pm Monday to Friday. Exchange rates vary from bank to bank, and a hefty minimum charge is levied on travellers' cheques. Cash can be obtained from banks, automatic cash dispensers and money changers (Multibanco), of which there are many in the Baixa and around the Rossio.

At Banco Espirito Santo e Comercial de Lisboa, in Rossio Square, you can change money on Saturdays. You can also change money at the airport.

Books

A few suggested books to enhance your stay in Lisbon might include:
Luis Vaz de Camões, *The Lusiads*
Rodney Gallop *Portugal – A Book of Folkways*
Almeida Garrett *Travels in My Homeland*
Jan Read *The Moors in Spain and Portugal*
John Ure *Henry the Navigator*
Edite Vieira *A Taste of Portugal*

Camping

You can camp all year round in Lisbon at the Parque de Campismo Municipal, in the Monsanto Park (Estrada de Circuncalaçao ☎ **21 760 20 61**, Fax 21 760 74 74). You can also camp at Cascais, Mafra and Sintra. To obtain lists of camping sites, contact the Portuguese Tourist Office, which publishes a list of state-owned and private sites, each graded one to four stars. Camping outside official sites is not permitted. An international camping *carnet* is obligatory and booking is advisable in high season. Contact the **Federação Portuguesa de Campismo-Caravanismo**, Avenida Col. Eduardo Galhardo ☎ **21 812 69 00**, Fax 21 812 69 18.

Car Rental
It is worth hiring a car to go outside Lisbon and visit attractions in the surrounding area. The main hire agencies are represented in Lisbon and at the airport:
Avis ☎ **21 346 11 71**
Europcar ☎ **21 940 77 90**
Hertz ☎ **21 942 63 00** or **800 23 82 38**

To rent a car in Portugal you must be at least 21 (some companies stipulate 23) and have held a full driving licence for a year. The rental contract, a valid driving licence, valid vehicle insurance and your passport must be carried at all times. Failure to produce any of these at the request of the authorities may result in an on-the-spot fine.

Make sure you have comprehensive insurance and check that the tyres, including the spare, are in good repair and the brakes work before setting off. *See also* **Driving**

Children
Children are welcomed in Portugal. They get large reductions on public transport and generally travel free up to 4 or 5 years. Museums are free to children under 11 or 12. In hotels, children under 8 pay half price if they sleep in the same room as their parents.

Visiting museums can be tiring or boring for children, but fortunately Lisbon has a number of places which are likely to interest them, such as: the **Vasco de Gama Aquarium** (Museu Aquarío), located at the Dáfundo to the north of Lisbon; **Monsanto Park**, which has play areas and two swimming pools; the **Puppet Museum** (Museu das Marionetas) in Alfama and the **Jardim Zoológico**, which also has a very fine park. Of course, a visit to the **Parque das Nações**, with its cable car, playground (Parque do Gil), gardens with fountains, the spectacular Oceanário and the many other attractions is a must!

Finally, at Sintra, the **Museu do Brinquedo** (Toy Museum), located in a fire station, offers both a beautiful collection and a multimedia play area.

Clothing

The climate is generally hot and sunny, but it is advisable to take a sweater, even in summer, as the evenings can turn cool, with breezes coming in off the Atlantic. Smarter clothing is required in some of the more expensive hotels and restaurants.

Women's Sizes

UK	8	10	12	14		16	18
Portugal	34	36	38	40		42	44
US	6	8	10	12		14	16

Men's Suits

UK/US	36	38	40	42		44	46
Portugal	46	48	50	52		54	56

Men's Shirts

UK/US	14	14.5	15	15.5	16	16.5	17
Portugal	36	37	38	39/40	41	42	43

Men's Shoes

UK	7	7.5	8.5	9.5		10.5	11
Portugal	41	42	43	44		45	46
US	8	8.5	9.5	10.5		11.5	12

Women's Shoes

UK	4.5	5	5.5	6		6.5	7
Portugal	38	38	39	39		40	41
US	6	6.5	7	7.5		8	8.5

Consulates

These can be located at the following addresses:

Australian Embassy
Avenida da Liberdade
244–2 e4, 1200 Lisboa
☎ 21 65 41 61

British Embassy
Rua São Domingos à Lapa
35–37, 1200 Lisboa
☎ 21 396 11 91

British Consulate
Largo Francisco A. Mauricio
7-1, 8500 Portimão
☎ (082) 23071/27057

Canadian Embassy
Avenida da Liberdade 144,
4th Floor, 1250 Lisboa
☎ 21 347 48 92

Irish Embassy
Rua da Imprensa 1,
4th Floor, Lisboa
☎ 21 66 15 69

US
Avenida Forças Armadas,
1600 Lisboa
☎ 21 727 33 00

Crime

There is no need to be unduly concerned about crime in Lisbon, but it is advisable to take sensible precautions.
• Carry as little money and as few credit cards as possible, and leave any valuables in the hotel safe.
• Carry wallets and purses in secure pockets or wear a money belt, and carry handbags across your body or firmly under your arm.
• Cars, particularly hire cars, are targeted by thieves, so never leave your car unlocked,

and always remove any items of value.

• If you do have anything stolen, report it immediately to the local police and collect a copy of the report so that you can make an insurance claim.

• If your passport is stolen, report it to your consulate or embassy at once.

Customs and Entry Regulations

The Single European market ensures considerable tax-free allowances for travellers from EU countries, and there is no limit on the transfer of goods for personal use. Those under 17 years of age do not have an allowance. Otherwise the limits are as follows:

Cigarettes 800 (non EU or bought at duty-free shops 200)
Spirits 10 litres (non EU or bought at duty-free shops 1 litre)
Fortified wine 20 litres (non EU or bought at duty-free shops 2 litres)
Wine 90 litres (non EU or bought at duty-free shops 2 litres)
Beer 110 litres (EU only)

Disabled Visitors

Holidays and Travel Abroad: A Guide to Europe is available from RADAR, 12 City Forum, 250 City Road, London EC1V 8AF

Picking grapes for port wine in the Duoro Valley.

☎ **0171 250 3222** (open from 10am-4pm). It contains advice and information about accommodation, transport, services, equipment and tour operators in Europe. The Holiday Care Service is available to advise British disabled people wishing to travel abroad, and can be contacted on ☎ **01293 774535**.

Tripsocope ☎ **0181 994 9294** give advice about all aspects of travel and transport for the disabled and elderly in Portugal, and can offer detailed help with planning journeys, equipment hire, etc.

A brochure published by the

Portuguese government for disabled travellers can be obtained from the Secretariado Nacional de Rehabilitação, Ave Conde de Valbom 63 ☎ 21 793 65 17.

Turintegra (Pr Dr Fernando Amado, Lisboa ☎ 21 859 53 32) makes travel arrangements for disabled people.

Even though there are no special facilities on public transport for the disabled, a flexible minibus service is available every day from 7am to midnight. The fare is the same as for public transport, but the only problem is that you must book 48 hours in advance ☎ 21 758 56 76.

Driving
Driving in Lisbon is difficult.

The roads are narrow, there are many one-way streets, parking places are few and bottlenecks are impossible to avoid. Even if you travel to Lisbon by car, leave it where you are staying, if possible in a secure parking area.

If you do drive in the city, the Baixa has underground parking (Praça dos Restauradores, Rossio, Praça do Comércio), but parking is almost impossible in the small streets of the Bairro Alto and Alfama.

At tourist sites, young people (often drug addicts) will indicate where to park. It is the custom to give them a coin. In addition to this, do not forget to put money in the parking meter, if there is one.

Always have with you the car's registration document (or rental contract if a hire car), a valid national driving licence (or international driving licence if you are not a member of an EU country), valid vehicle insurance (a green card is no longer compulsory for members of EU countries, but is strongly advisable if you are driving your own car) and your passport. Failure to produce any of these on request of the authorities may result in an on-the-spot fine.

The police will also readily impose on-the-spot fines for not wearing seat belts in the front and rear seats and for driving while drunk.

Driving in Portugal is on the right-hand side and traffic approaching from the right has priority. Speed limits, clearly marked on the roads, are as follows:
• Maximum on motorways 120 kph/75 mph (minimum 40 kph/25 mph)
• Maximum in built-up areas 50 kph (31 mph)
• Maximum on other roads 90 kph (56 mph)

Electric Current
The standard current throughout Portugal is 220V, although you may still find 110V in older establishments. Sockets are the circular, two-pin variety so you will need to take an adaptor for any of your own appliances.

Emergencies
Police, fire and ambulance are all on the same number: ☎ 115.

Excursions and Tours
see **p.88**

Health
British citizens should obtain the Form E111 (available from Post Offices) which entitles the holder to free urgent treatment in other EU countries. On arrival in Portugal, exchange the form at the **Segurança Social** for a book of coupons. It is advisable to take out comprehensive medical insurance.

Pharmacies (*farmácias*) are open normal shop hours (*see* **Opening Hours**) and one branch in each town remains open until late in the evening – its address is posted in the windows of all other pharmacies and in the local newspapers or ☎ 118

Language
Portuguese is the official language in Lisbon, but English, French and Spanish are often spoken. As in any country, however, an attempt at the native language will be appreciated. A few basic phrases are given overleaf.

Lost Property
If you lose something on public transport, apply to the Carris Company, whose office is alongside the Santa Justa lift ☎ 21 363 93 43.

For property lost anywhere other than on public transport, go to the Central Lost Property Office: Departamento de perdidos e achados da PSP, Praça Cidade Salazar, Lote 180r/c, Olivais Sul ☎ 21 853

Good morning/**Bom dia**
Good evening/**Boa tarde**
Goodbye/**Adeus**
Please/**Por favor**
Thank you (if you are male)/**Obrigado**
Thank you (if you are female)/**Obrigada**
Yes/**Sim**
No/**Não**
Do you speak English?/**Fala inglês?**
Where is .. ?/**Onde é ..?**
How much is .. ?/**Quanto é ..?**
I would like ../**Queria ...**
I don't understand/**Não compreendo**

54 03 (open Monday to Friday, 9am-noon and 2-6pm).

Maps and Guides

Michelin publishes a range of maps, including **No 990** (1/1 000 000) which covers Spain and Portugal, and a map of Portugal, **No 940** (1/400 000), together with a *Spain-Portugal Road Atlas* (1/400 000) which also includes town plans.

When travelling round Lisbon, use Michelin map **No 39 Lisboa**, at a scale of 1/10 000. This includes an alphabetical list of streets, main thoroughfares and one-way streets, the main public buildings and many points of tourist interest.

The *Michelin Green Guide Portugal* includes maps of the various districts of Lisbon and detailed descriptions of its principal monuments, museums and other interesting sights.

The *Michelin Red Guide* booklet *Hotels and Restaurants Portugal* offers a wide selection of hotels and restaurants, classified by district, comfort and quality of cooking, updated every year.

Money

The unit of currency in Portugal is the *escudo* (Esc.), which now benefits from a fixed exchange rate for the Euro zone. A Euro equals 200.482 escudos and one escudo is 0.0049879 Euros. The escudo is divided into 100 *centavos*. The monetary symbol is the dollar sign ($), placed between the escudo amount and the centavos, e.g., 20$50 is 20 escudos and 50 centavos. Banknotes come in denominations of 500, 1 000, 2 000, 5 000 and 10 000 escudos; coins in $50, 1$, 2$50, 5, 10, 20, 50, 100 and 200 escudos. One thousand escudos is known as a *conto*.

There is no limit to the amount of escudos or foreign currency which may be taken into Portugal, but on leaving the country no more than 100 000$ per person in local currency and/or travellers' cheques, and no more than the equivalent of 500 000$ in foreign currency may be taken out. Foreign visitors entering Portugal must have a minimum of 10 000$ (or equivalent in another currency) and a further 2 000$ for each day of their stay.

International credit and debit cards are widely accepted in the resorts, and money and travellers' cheques can be changed at banks and many hotels (you will need your passport). Many banks also have automatic cash dispensers which accept international credit cards.

If your credit card is lost or stolen, call immediately: Cartão de Credito S.O.S.
☎ **21 357 39 08**

American Express
☎ **(00) 331 4777 7000**
Diners Club
☎ **(00) 331 4906 1750**
Eurocard/Mastercard
☎ **(00) 331 4567 8484**
Visa ☎ **(00)331 4277 1190** (or **33 5442 1212** in the provinces)

Museums
The **Lisboa Card** – sold at various places, including the airport, the Tourist Office, the main post office (Rua Jardim do Regedor 50), at Jerónimos Monastery and the National Museum of Ancient Art – includes entry to 26 museums and monuments, reduced prices for other museums and for cruises on the Tagus, and free travel on the underground, buses, trams and funiculars. It is valid for 24 hours (1 900-750 for children), 48 hours (3 100-1 100$) or 72 hours (4 000-1 550$). Note, however, that most museums are free on Sundays and closed Mondays. Normal entrance prices vary between 200$ and 500$.

Newspapers
All major international newspapers and magazines are available on the newsstands, often on the day of publication. The main dailies are the *Diario de Noticias, Correio da*

Manha, Público, and the weeklies include *O Expresso* and *O Independente*.

The *Agenda Cultural* provides a programme of all artistic and cultural activities every month. It is available free from the Tourist Office and some hotels.

Follow me Lisboa is a free bilingual Portuguese/English weekly, filled with practical and cultural information. It is found in cultural establishments and in some bars.

Opening Hours

Shops are generally open from 9am-1pm and 3-7pm, Monday to Friday, and 9am-1pm on Saturdays, except for a few in the Rua Augusta and at the main tourist sites.

Supermarkets are generally open from 8am-8pm on weekdays, with some opening on Sundays.

The **Almoreiras Commercial Centre** (Avenida Engenheiro Duarte Pacheco) is open from 10am-10pm every day; the complex includes 300 small shops, a supermarket, 55 restaurants and cinema complexes. It appears very small now, when compared to the huge **Centro Vasco da Gama** built at the entrance to the Parque das Nações, near the Oriente Underground.

Markets usually start early and pack up by 1pm. Large shopping centres are open daily from 10am-1am.

Museums and galleries are generally open from 10am-6pm, although some close between noon and 2pm. Most are closed on Mondays.
See also **Banks** and **Post Offices**

Police

The Guarda Fiscal are the police responsible for day to day law and order, traffic offences and tourist assistance. They can be recognised by their blue and grey uniforms.

The Polícia Judiciária, clad in navy blue uniforms, are concerned with violent and large-scale crime in Portugal.

Post Offices

The main post office is on Praça dos Restaudores, and is open Monday to Fridays, from 8am-10pm, and 9am-6pm on weedends and public holidays. Other post offices are generally open from 8.30am-6pm Monday to Friday. *Poste restante* mail can be sent to the Central Correios, Praça do Comércio. Proof of identity will be needed on collection.

Letter boxes and phone booths are red.

Stamps *(selos)* are sold in post offices and shops where the sign CTT Correios is displayed. It costs 95$ to send a postcard to European countries.

Public Holidays

The national public holidays are listed below.

New Year's Day: 1 January

Shrove Tuesday: late February/early March

Good Friday: end March/early April

Liberation Day: 25 April

Labour Day: 1 May

Corpus Christi: End May/early June

National Day: 10 June

Feast Day of Lisbon's Patron Saint: 13 June

Assumption of the Virgin: 15 August

Republic Day: 5 October

All Saints' Day: 1 November

Independence Day: 1 December

Day of Our Lady: 8 December

Christmas Day: 25 December

Religion

Portugal is predominantly a Roman Catholic country and Masses are held daily in local churches. Services of most Christian denominations are conducted in English in Lisbon. Details from the tourist office and larger hotels.

Telephones

Payphones can be found all over the city. Many are coin operated, but a large number also take phonecards. There are two types of **phonecards**: *Portugal Telecom* (around Lisbon and Porto) and *Credifone*. These cards can be bought in Portugal Telecom shops, at post offices, certain kiosks and newsstands. The cards are available in 50 units (555$), 100 units (1 111$) or 150 units (1 624$). You can also call from booths in post offices, where you pay at the desk at the end of the call. The cost is the same as a payphone. Calls from hotels are much more expensive.

Country codes:

Australia: ☎ 00 61

Canada: ☎ 00 1

Ireland: ☎ 00 353

New Zealand: ☎ 64

UK: ☎ 00 44

USA: ☎ 00 1

For an English-speaking operator ☎ 098. To phone Portugal from the UK, ☎ 00 351 + 34 + area code + number.

Area codes:

For calls from the provinces to Lisbon, ☎ 21 followed by 7 numbers; from Lisbon to the provinces, dial a 3-number code (**262** to Óbidos, **244** to Batalha, **261** to Mafra, **262** to Alcobaça; Cascais and Sintra have the same code as Lisbon – **21**).

Useful numbers:
International directory
enquiries ☎ 118
Emergencies ☎ 112
Collect calls ☎ 120
Police ☎ 21 346 61 41 and
☎ 21 347 47 30
Pharmacy on duty ☎ 118
International telegrams ☎ 182
Automatic wake-up calls ☎ 161

Time Difference
From the last Sunday in
September to the last Sunday
in March, Portugal is
Greenwich Mean Time (GMT)
plus one hour. During the
summer clocks go forward one
hour (in accordance with
British Summer Time), and so
are two hours ahead of GMT.

Tipping
In most hotels, restaurants and
cafés service is already
included in the bill; if not, 10
per cent is usual or an extra tip
can be given for special
service. Taxi drivers and hair-
dressers expect a 10 per cent
tip, and porters and hotel staff
are used to a small gratuity.

Toilets
Public toilets are not readily
available; those in a bar or
restaurant can be used by the
general public, but it is polite
to ask first, and to have a drink
afterwards. The cleanest facilities tend to be in hotels. Ladies
are marked *Senhoras*, and
Gentlemen *Senhores*, or
Homens.

Tourist Information Offices
The **Portuguese National
Tourist Office (ICEP)**, Palcio
Foz, Praça dos Restauradores,
is open Mondays to Saturdays
from 9am-8pm, and Sundays
from 10am-6pm, ☎ 21 342 52
31 and 21 346 36 43. There is
also an office at Avenida
Conde Valbom, 30-4° ☎ 21
352 58 10 and another at the
airport, ☎ 21 849 36 89.
**Portuguese National Tourist
Offices abroad:**
Canada 60 Bloor Street West,
Suite 1 005, Toronto,
Ontario M4W 3B8
☎ **(416) 921 7376**
Ireland Knocksinna House,
Knocksinna, Fox Rock,
Dublin 18
☎ **(01) 289 3569**
UK 22–25a Sackville Street,
London W1X 1DE
☎ **(0171) 494 1441**
US 590 Fifth Avenue, 4th
Floor, New York, NY 10036
☎ **(212) 354 4403/4**

The municpality of Lisbon has
set up the **Quiosque Cultural
de S. Mamede**, in the Príncipe
Real district, providing information on the city's cultural
events. To obtain tickets for

A tram in the colours of Expo 98 in Praça Comércio.

theatre performances, concerts, football matches etc. the easiest thing to do is to go to the **ABEP kiosk**, Praça dos Restauradores ☎ 21 342 53 60.

Transport

Taxis are cheap, apart from the initial charge (250$), and are fast. However, be careful, especially at night, to check the route taken, and when getting into the taxi check the meter has been set back to zero. Generally, taxis are beige, but some old ones are black with a green roof. A red light on the roof indicates that they are free, a green that they are occupied.
Rádio Táxis de Lisboa
☎ 21 811 90 00/90 19/90 60 or 21 815 18 67.

Teletáxi ☎ 21 811 11 00
Public transport in Lisbon (above ground) is operated by the Carris Company.
 Buses and **trams** are frequent and serve all Lisbon districts, generally running from 7am-1am. The funiculars stop at 11pm. The last no 45 bus (Cais do Sodré, Baixa, Av. da Liberdade) leaves at 1.55am.

Visitors should try to use the trams (*eléctricos*) which, rattling through the narrow streets with a clank of iron, are part of the Lisbon scene. Despite the advertisements that cover their sides, they have retained their charm. The 15 and 28 follow interesting routes: the **15** (Praça da Figueira/Algés) passes by the Praça do Comércio, the Coach Museum, the Jéronimos Monastery, the Maritime Museum, the Monument to the Discoveries and the Tower of Belém; the **28** (Martim Moniz/Prazeres) goes from the Jardim de Estrela to the Graça district, passing the Bairro Alto, Praça do Comércio, the Cathedral and the São Vicente de Fora church. Tourist trams follow special routes in summer; information is available from the Tourist Office.

You can buy tickets on the buses and trams. **Tourist Tickets** (*Passe Turistico*), valid for one, three, four or seven days, offer unlimited travel on all public transport, including funiculars and the Santa Justa lift. To obtain a ticket you must show proof of identity at the kiosks marked 'Venda de Passe' in the Praça da Figueira, the Cais do Sodré or at the Santa Justa lift. Ask for a **transport map** (*Planta dos Transportes Públicas da Carris*) at the same time. Another option is the **Lisboa Card**, valid for 24, 48 or 72 hours, which gives you access to the buses, trams and underground (operated by another company and where the Carris tickets for buses and trams are not accepted) and free tickets or reductions to a certain number of museums and monuments.

The **underground** runs from 6.30am-1am. The system has been modernised and the trains are very frequent. There are four lines, identified by their colours and called Gaivota (blue), Girassol (yellow), Caravela (green) and Oriente (red).

Contemporary artists have decorated some stations, such as *Alto dos Moinhos* (Júlio Pomar), which also houses the Music Museum and sometimes holds concerts, *Parque* (decorated with blue azulejos and sculptures and displaying aphorisms from Nietzche, Lao-Tseu and Pessôa), or *Rato, Cidade Universitária, Pontinha, Carnide* or *Picoas*.

Launches (*cacilheiros*) cross the Tagus every 10 minutes. They leave from the quay near the Praça do Comércio, from the Cais do Sodré, and from the Praça A. de Albuquerque at Belém.

Trains International lines and those serving the north of the country operate from Santa Apolónia Station. Trains for Estoril and Cascais (approximately every 20 minutes until 2.30am) run from Cais do Sodré Station, while Rossio Station serves the north-western suburbs, including Sintra.

INDEX

INDEX